# SHORT BIKE RIDES ON CAPE COD, NANTUCKET AND THE VINEYARD

Jane Griffith and Edwin Mullen

The Globe Pequot Press

Old Chester Road
Chester, Connecticut

# Introduction

These short rides provide an opportunity to explore Cape Cod and the Islands in a unique and rewarding way: By bicycle on hassle-free, planned tours. The rides are from seven to twenty-seven miles long and range in difficulty from the flat terrain of The Cape Cod Canal to the hills of Martha's Vineyard. They can be ridden in a few hours, but to experience all the pleasures of the ride allow *at least* a half a day. Don't let age deter you from taking these rides: We are forty-three and fifty-three, and children from age ten have also done the rides and had a good time. To ensure your enjoyment, take some precautions as outlined in the section on SAFETY, and some good equipment: For picnicking and swimming, pannier bags on your rear rack and handlebar bags are indispensable. As to the bike itself, we recommend a good ten speed model—the best you can afford. A three speed would be all right for the flat country rides but would take the enjoyment out of the others—and that's what it's all about.

## Cape Cod

This arm of Massachusetts, site of the pilgrims' first landfall, is about seventy-five miles long and has over three hundred miles of coast line. Formed some ten thousand years ago by action of the retreating glacier, the Cape is a bony, sandy outcropping punctuated by bluffs, marshes, and ponds (probably created when dense ice chunks amid the debris melted away).

The Cape was settled within a couple of decades of Plymouth, and the colonists took to fishing, hunting and haying the salt meadows. Settlers also denuded the Cape of its trees for housing, ship building, firewood and pasture land. The cutting over, combined with the natural wash and blow dry the flora and terrain absorb from relentless waves and winds, explains the Cape's unique and fascinating appearance: rugged but right.

## Cape Cod National Seashore

The Cape Cod National Seashore was created in 1961 by Act of Congress. Its 27,000 acres located in six towns are under

National Parks Service supervision. About two-thirds of the acres are owned by the Seashore; the rest of the acreage remains in private hands or is held by the towns, but physical changes to these properties are strictly controlled.

The two Visitors' Centers, Province Lands and Salt Pond, are open from 9:00 - 6:00, seven days a week, during the season. Salt Pond offers an illuminated table top map of the Cape, a brief introductory film, and dioramas illustrating the history and geology of the Cape, as well as trail guides and facilities. Province Lands Visitor's Center provides one of the Cape's most beautiful overlooks. Trail guides, exhibits, orientation talks and facilities are available. Camping is not allowed in the Seashore. The dunes, flora and fauna must remain undisturbed. Lifeguard service and public facilities are available at the following beaches: Coast Guard, Nauset Light, Marconi, Head of Headow, Race Point, and Herring Cove. The Seashore extends along the Cape's entire Atlantic shore, from its southernmost point below Chatham to Provincetown. Unforgettable!

## Martha's Vineyard

In 1602, wild grapes grew abundantly on the Island, and in that year explorer Bartholomew Gosnold, who had a young daughter named Martha, took note of it, and made this vineyard, here on the other side of the world, her namesake.

Colonists came in 1642 to establish Edgartown, having bought the whole lashup, unbeknownst to the Indian inhabitants who had lived there compatibly time immemorial, for forty pounds from two gentlemen in England. The community prospered with fishing, whaling, sheep herding, dairying and boat building; new settlements were established. The Revolution disrupted the Islanders' lives and economy, but recovery was complete by 1820 when the whaling and building booms were at their height. The triple whammy of the Gold Rush, the Civil War and the discovery of petroleum would have resulted in a bleak future indeed had it not been for the timely burgeoning of summer religious camp meetings which prompted a land development boom. To this day tourism is the Island's principal source of income, causing the population to soar from some seven thousand year around residents to about seventy thousand in the season.

With that figure in mind, we exhort you not to bring a car here in the summer. Congestion is terrible and parking is ridiculous. From May through September: The bike's the thing! Bring your own, or rent one, and take the bus in between treks. (Shuttles operate back and forth from Vineyard Haven, Oak Bluffs and Edgartown twice an hour in season.) Ferries bring people to Vineyard Haven from Woods Hole and New Bedford, and to Oak Bluffs from Falmouth, Hyannis and New Bedford. (Only the Woods Hole ferries carry cars.) No camping is allowed on the beaches. There are three commercial camp grounds. Oak Bluffs and Edgartown are wet; the rest of the Island is dry but you may bring your own. Beaches open to the public include (1) in Vineyard Haven: Owen Park Beach; (2) in Oak Bluffs: Joseph Sylvia State Beach, and the Town Beach; (3) in Edgartown: Katama (South) Beach; (4) in Chappaquiddick: East Beach; (5) in Chilmark: Menemsha Town Beach and Menemsha Hills; (6) in Gay Head: Lobsterville Beach. The Martha's Vineyard State Forest Bike Trail (which isn't written up elsewhere in this book) provides the cyclist with fourteen miles of bike paths around and through this four thousand acre pine, oak and spruce forest. A good starting point is the Youth Hostel on the West Tisbury Rd. As the forest is smack in the middle of Martha's Vineyard, however, all roads lead there! You can pick up a map of the Trail anywhere on the Island.

## Nantucket

Nantucket, thirty miles south of Cape Cod, was created when a glacier melted away dropping the immense load of earth and debris which shaped the Island's width and length of three miles by fifteen.

Martha's Vineyard's discoverer Gosnold also came here in 1602, but the Island wasn't settled until some sixty years later when the Quakers came. The Indians were kindly disposed—which was apparently unfortunate for them: By the middle 1800s they had left or died off and their culture vanished from Nantucket.

From 1712, when the first sperm whale was done in, until the middle 1800s, when the Fire of 1846 gutted the town, and combined with the Civil War and the period's economic developments to end the bubble, Nantucket prospered and the Captains built their Georgian, Federal and Greek Revival mansions, leaving some four hundred houses here which are more than a hundred years old.

Nantucket's present economy depends largely on tourism, but commercial fishing is still a significant activity. In a unique way Nantucket depends on the past to attract people here, and depends on the present to keep them coming. The Island's exotic whaling history captures the imagination, but its sun, sand, flora and moors bring one sharply into the present.

Reach Nantucket by ferry from Woods Hole (two and a half hours, cars allowed) or Hyannis (two hours). We urge you not to take a car there. You will have a time finding a place to put it, and the entire Island is exhuberantly and easily reached by bicycle. (Bring your own or rent one here.)

Nantucket doesn't allow camping out or sleeping in vehicles.

Public beaches are Jettie's Beach, Surfside, Cisco, 'Sconset, Dionis and Madaket.

See you on the road!

Jane Griffith
Edwin Mullen
New Haven, Ct.

# TABLE OF CONTENTS

# Safety

Riding the roads of Massachusetts on a bicycle can be dangerous—if you are careless with your equipment or with yourself. Bicycles are legal vehicles in Massachusetts, entitled to use all roads except limited access highways. The Massachusetts Bicycle Laws state that bicyclists must:

Obey all traffic signs, lights and other regulations.

Ride with traffic, *never* the wrong way.

Give clear hand signals.

Yield to pedestrians.

Ride single file.

Where bicycle paths are provided along highways they should be used.

Additional tips for the crowded roads of the Cape, Martha's Vineyard and Nantucket: Don't ride on sidewalks in town centers, walk your bike when going against traffic on a one-way street, call out and slow down when approaching horses.

Secure your bike against theft by using one of the new bolt-cutter-proof locks. This is a *must*! Take along a few simple tools: A screwdriver, pliers and an adjustable wrench. Take a rag in case your chain really "derails". Make sure that all nuts are tight and that the derailleurs and brakes are working properly. Check your bike before you leave. No matter how long you've been riding use a check list before each ride. The one that we use is printed here.

# Check List

1. Brakes
2. Derailleurs
3. Wheel nuts
4. Tires
5. Light
6. Horn
7. Bolt-cutter-proof lock
8. Tool kit
9. Rag
10. Water bottle
11. Front and rear bags
12. First aid kit
13. Insect repellant
14. Sunglasses
15. Head protection
16. Wash-N-Dry towelettes
17. Half roll of toilet paper
18. Ground cloth (for picnicking)
19. Food and drink
20. Towel and bathing suit
21. Money
22. Short Bike Rides on Cape Cod, Nantucket & the Vineyard

# 1   Cape Cod Canal - Sandwich

**No. of miles:** 17
**Approximate pedalling time:** 2 hours, 15 minutes
**Terrain:** Flat
**Surface:** Good
**Things to see:** The Canal, Sandwich Glass Museum, Sandwich
Town Hall, Dexter Grist Mill, Hoxie House, Heritage
Plantation, Shawmee Pond, Shawmee Crowell State Park.
**How to get there:** Coming from the west on 6 and 28, take 28 at
Buzzard's Bay and cross the Bourne Bridge. At the traffic
circle, bear right and take the road that goes downhill, back
towards the Canal. At the "T" intersection turn right and go
under the bridge and then turn immediately left and go to the
parking lot at the Canal side.


This lovely and varied ride starts at the Cape Cod Canal, just
under the Bourne Bridge. There is a parking lot here, and
restrooms (during the summer season only) maintained by the
U.S. Army Corps. of Engineers.

Leave your motorized bike-carrier here, mount up and turn
right onto the paved access road which runs along the Canal.
This road is for government vehicles (a rare sight) and bicycles
only.

Follow the contour of the canal, which, in the warm months,
is full of boats large and small. The current is swift, six-seven
knots at times, and often the sailboats seem to be standing still.
Near the end of the Canal you'll come to the enormous NETCO
electrical power generating plant. Skirt right around it on the
Canal side, and arrive at the Sandwich-Cape Cod Canal Marina.
Go to the parking lot, turn left through it, and continue bearing
left. By the large Coast Guard Station and the big Canal fish
market, where fresh fish is unloaded and prepared for ship-
ment, bear right. Just past here is a gate which you just go
around, continuing to the very end of the Canal where there is a
small beach. When we rode there (in the late fall) the moon was
rising over Cape Cod Bay, the navigation lights were flashing,
and we could see the buoys marking the entrance to the Canal.
A beautiful sight!

Turn around and come back along the roadway to Coast
Guard Rd. Turn left, past the Coast Guard Station on your right.

(Continued Page 14)

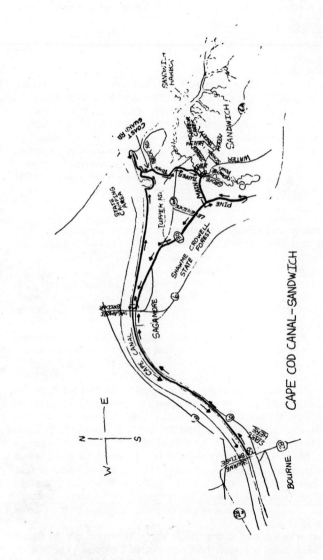

CAPE COD CANAL-SANDWICH

**Directions for the ride:**

- Start from the parking lot at the Canal, under the Bourne Bridge, on the Cape side.
- Go out onto the Canal access road and turn right.
- Ride along the access road to the Sandwich Cape Cod Canal Marina.
- Go through the Marina parking lot and left to the very end of the canal.
- Return on the same roadway to Coast Guard Rd.
- Turn left on Coast Guard Rd. to Town Neck Rd.
- Turn right on Town Neck Rd. to Tupper Rd.
- Turn left on Tupper Rd. to Main St. (Rte. 130).
- Turn left on Main St. (Rte. 130) to the historic sites.
- Return on Rte. 130 to Pine St.
- Turn left on Pine St. to Heritage Plantation.
- Return via Pine St. to Rte. 130.
- Turn left on Rte. 130 to Rte. 6A.
- Turn left on Rte. 6A to the fork with Rte. 6
- Bear right on Rte. 6, where the sign says 6 AND SAGAMORE VILLAGE to the Rte. 6 bridge over the Canal.
- Turn right at the bridge (under it) to the Canal access road.
- Turn left on the access road and return to your starting place.

At the stop sign turn right onto Town Neck Rd. Just over the railroad tracks come to a "T" with Tupper Rd. Turn left onto Tupper. Stay on Tupper past Rte. 6A, to the tiny center of Sandwich.

In this small area there are six places of interest to see. Turn left onto Rte. 130, on the left is the Sandwich Glass Museum; just across the street, on Shawmee Pond, is the Dexter Grist Mill; and, up Rte. 130 a bit, on the right, on the shore of the pond, is the Hoxie House.

The Dexter Grist Mill was built around 1650 and still grinds corn meal which can be purchased here. The mill is open from mid-June to September ($.75 for adults; $.50 for children).

The Hoxie House, a classic Salt Box, was built in 1637 which would make it the oldest house on Cape Cod. It was acquired by the town and beautifully restored. It is also open from mid-June to September, ($.50 adults; $.35 children). Shawmee Pond is a jewel of a pond, teeming with wild geese, ducks and swans in season. It is an artificial lake created around 1633 by the settlers who built a dam to provide water power for the mill. In April the fish ladder is packed with thousands of leaping herring (alewives) coming upstream to spawn.

After you have enjoyed all of these goodies, (and if you have some time and a few dollars left), turn around and head south on 130. In about a half mile you come to Pine St. Turn left and go uphill for one mile until you come to Heritage Plantation. This is a large place, dedicated to antique America. It consists of beautiful gardens, a working windmill, a 1912 Carousel, a round Shaker Barn, antique automobiles, etc. It is open from 10:00 a.m. to 4:00 p.m. from May 1 to mid-October ($2.50 adults; $.75 children).

When you are ready to leave, return (downhill this time) to Rte. 130. Turn left on 130, past an old sprawling cemetery on the right, past Shawmee-Crowell State Park (one of two on Cape Cod with campsites—first come, first served!). When you arrive at the junction with 6A go left onto it, but you have to turn right and then left to do so. At the fork of Rte. 6A and 6, bear right where the sign says ROUTE 6 AND SAGAMORE VILLAGE. Pass through Sagamore Village and you'll soon find yourself at the Rte. 6 bridge over the Canal. The route parallels the Canal here. Turn right at the bridge and go directly to the access road along the Canal. Turn left and re-trace the bike route the three and a half miles back to your starting place at the Bourne Bridge.

# 2 Bourne

**Number of Miles:** 18.5
**Approximate pedalling time:** 2 hours, 15 minutes
**Surface:** Good
**Terrain:** Varied, long flat stretches, some hills
**Things to see:** Cape Cod Canal, Cataumet Methodist Church, Aptuxet Trading Post and Windmill, communities of Bourne, Monument Beach, Pocasset, Cataumet and Megansett (North Falmouth).
**How to get there:** Take Rte. 28 across the Cape Cod Canal on the Bourne Bridge. At the rotary immediately after crossing the bridge, turn right. Promptly bear right again on Freeman St. and keep bearing right until you're directly under the bridge; then turn left onto a short unmarked road leading directly to the Canal and the parking area.

The ride begins in the parking lot on the east side of the Canal under the Bourne Bridge. There are picnic tables and restrooms here. These facilities as well as the Canal and its "Tow Path" are maintained by the Corps. of Engineers. Mount up and go left on the Canal Service Road heading south. This is a hard packed gravel road. After a mile, at the site of the railroad bridge, you'll reach the end of this leg. Walk your bike down the embankment and over the tracks to the parking lot. Ride through the lot and alongside the Canal on Jefferson St. to the Point; here, you're almost at the south end of the canal.

Now retrace the route to the parking lot, turn right on Bell Rd. and ride out to Shore Road. Turn right on Shore Rd. Bear left at the fork where there is a small traffic island. Pass Old Dam Rd. on the left. At a sign which points to POCASSET - 2 MILES, Shore Rd. appears to "T;" in fact, it jogs right and then left in front of the railroad station. There's a Cumberland Farms store here. Continue on Shore Rd. You're now in the community of Monument Beach. Upon reaching the Pocasset River stop at the bridge and take a look at the boats. This is a colorful, picturesque scene. There's a tiny harbor, but evidently the draft is deep because there are some enormous boars moored here. This area is called Pocasset.

Continue on Shore Rd. past Barlow's Landing. Just before going under an overpass, you'll see a sign to Cataumet's Marina
(Continued Page 18)

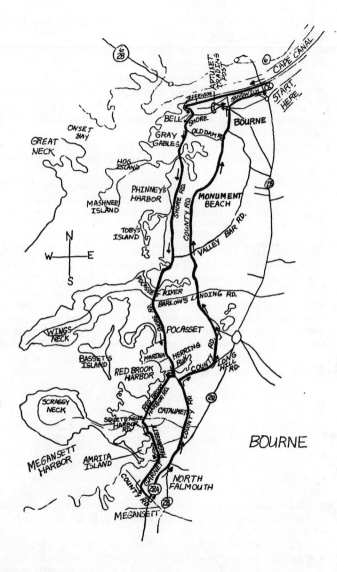

BOURNE

**Directions for the ride:**

- Start from the parking lot at the Canal, under the Bourne Bridge on the Cape side.
- Go to the Canal access road and turn left.
- Go to the end and down the embankment to Jefferson Rd. and onto the point.
- Return on Jefferson, through the parking lot to Bell Rd.
- Turn right on Bell Rd. to Shore Rd.
- Turn right on Shore Rd. and continue on it past Barlow's Landing Rd. to the road marked by a sign CATAUMET'S MARINA.
- Return up to Shore Rd. and turn right to Red Brook Harbor Rd.
- Turn right on Red Brook Harbor Rd. and continue on it when it changes to Squeteague Harbor Rd., to Meganset Rd.
- Bear right on Meganset Rd. which becomes Garnet Rd.
- Bear right on Garnet Rd. to County Rd.
- Turn left on County Rd. to Rte. 28A.
- Turn left on Rte. 28A to County Rd.
- Turn left on County Rd., all the way to the six way intersection with, among others, Shore Rd.
- Turn left on Shore Rd. to Aptuxet Rd.
- Turn right on Aptuxet Rd. to the Aptuxet Windmill and Trading Post complex.
- Return via Aptuxet Rd. and Shore Rd. to the six way intersection and take Sandwich Rd. to your starting place under the Bourne Bridge.

on your right. Ride in for a look at the boats and beautiful Red Brook Harbor. Then go under the underpass and up the hill— which is the first real hill we've encountered on this ride.

Take a hair pin right on Red Brook Harbor Rd. From the top of the hill you can see what used to be a windmill and is now a private house. Ride downhill to Parker's Boat Yard also located on Red Brook Harbor. This community is called Cataumet. There are numerous side roads leading to the water which you may want to explore. On this stretch you'll also see the cranberry bogs for which the Cape is justly famous. When you cross Scraggy Neck Rd., Red Brook Harbor Rd. becomes Squeteague Harbor Rd. At the fork, bear right staying on Squeteague Harbor Rd. At the intersection with Meganset Rd. bear right going slightly downhill on Meganset. Where there is a sign to AMARITA ISLAND, bear left. (Detour for a visit to Amarita if you like.) Here, Meganset Rd. becomes Garnet Rd., and you have just crossed into North Falmouth.

When you come to County Rd. turn left. Cross the railroad tracks. Shortly County Rd. with "T" into 28A where there is a sign saying CATAUMET. Turn left onto 28A. You'll go up a long grade and then bear off to your left again onto another branch of County Rd. where there is a sign to BARNSTABLE COUNTY HOSPITAL and CATAUMET. This starts as a gently rolling road but it becomes a fairly steep uphill as it takes you past a drive-in where you could pick up some fried clams or fish and chips before going on.

Continue on County Rd. at its intersection with Shore Rd. Soon you'll see the Cataumet Methodist Church and cemetery. The building dates from 1765. At the fork with Long Hill Rd. bear left, staying on County Rd. You'll pass by a shop for leaded and stained glass called The Tree House. As you may know, the Cape is rich with artisans in every craft, but this is one of the more unusual. In two more miles, after a couple of significant uphill grades, you'll reach a six way intersection where there will be signs to PROVIDENCE - BOSTON - MONUMENT BEACH. Turn left on Shore Rd. You'll be able to see the Aptuxet Windmill and Trading Post from Shore Rd. Turn right onto Aptuxet Rd. and head for the Windmill. Just beyond it is the Aptuxet Trading Post, originally built in 1627. There is a modest charge for the tour, which is offered from April 1 - October 31.

After your visit, return to the intersection and take Sandwich Rd. back to Bourne Bridge and your car.

# 3   West Barnstable - Sandy Neck

**Number of miles:** 10.3
**Approximate pedalling time:** 1 hour
**Terrain:** Varied
**Surface:** Good
**Things to see:** Country Store, West Parish Meeting House, Sandy Neck, Great Marshes.
**How to get there:** Travel east on 6A between Sandwich and Barnstable. Watch for a cemetery on your right. Turn right on Meetinghouse Way just beyond the cemetery. Cross the railroad tracks and park by the railroad station and post office.

Turn right on Meetinghouse Way to start your ride. You'll promptly pass the general store. We bought excellent cheese here for a roadside snack and enjoyed poking around the store. Go uphill. At the crest you'll get a view across the Great Marshes. There is a sidewalk along this two lane country road which you may use. When you come to a fork you'll see a sign BUZZARD'S BAY-6W; bear right, continuing on Meetinghouse Way.

Stop when you arrive at the West Parrish Meetinghouse to enjoy its serenity. The church (Congregational) was finished in 1719. Bear right on Cedar St. upon leaving the Meetinghouse. Pass Willow St. At Maple St. turn right. This is a gently rolling country road. Cross the railroad tracks and turn left on 6A.

Your route parallels the Great Marshes here. This extensive marsh comprises 3,000 acres. The early settlers used the "salt hay" collected here for such varied purposes as fodder, bedding, compost, thatching and insulation. If you're ever wondering what all those little wooden boxes are that dot such areas your curiosity can now be satisfied: they are bird houses for tree swallows attracted to the marsh to eat the insects, and wooden traps for horse flies (see Paul and Ruth Sadlier, SHORT WALKS ON CAPE COD AND MARTHA'S VINEYARD, Pequot Press, 1976).

Proceed on 6A to the fork with High St. Bear left up High St. and enjoy another view of the Great Marshes. When you come to Howland Ave., turn right and rejoin 6A. turning left. In short

(Continued Page 22)

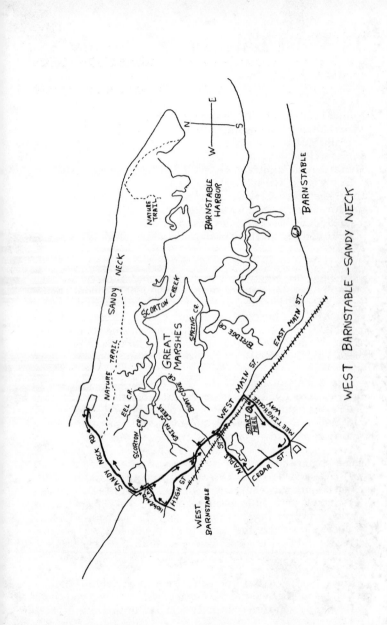

WEST BARNSTABLE – SANDY NECK

**Directions for the ride:**

- Park in West Barnstable at the West Barnstable Post Office on Meetinghouse Way.
- Go right (south) on Meetinghouse Way when you come out of the parking lot.
- Bear right at the fork to Buzzard's Bay.
- Bear right on Cedar St. at the Meetinghouse.
- Turn right on Maple St.
- Turn left on 6A.
- Bear left at the fork with High St.
- Turn right on Howland Ave.
- Turn left on 6A.
- Turn right on Sandy Neck Rd.
- Visit Sandy Neck Great Marsh and Beach.
- Return on Sandy Neck Rd.
- Turn left on 6A.
- Turn right on Meetinghouse Way and your car.

order, turn right on Sandy Neck Rd. Ride past marshes and sand dunes to the parking lot. From there go swimming, and hiking and birding on the marked trails winding through the six miles of Sandy Neck dunes. The beach, being on the bayside of the Cape, is a pebbly one, but nevertheless beautiful and inviting. This site is formally called Scortin Neck Beach and Nature Recreation Area. After your visit return to 6A on Sandy Neck Rd. Turn left and proceed on 6A until you come to Meeting-house Way. Turn right and return to your car in the railroad parking lot.

# 4 Barnstable - Cummaquid

**Number of miles:** 8.6
**Approximate pedalling time:** 1 hour
**Terrain:** Gently rolling
**Surface:** Good
**Things to see:** Colonial Court House, Sturgis Library, Trayser Memorial Museum.
**How to get there:** Take 6A to Barnstable and watch for the Sturgis Library on your left shortly after passing Rendezvous Rd. Park in the Library's parking lot or elsewhere near 6A if the lot is full.

Come out of the Library parking lot and head east on 6A (also called Cranberry Highway). You'll soon pass the Barnstable Comedy Club which is an amateur theater, and the Barnstable County Court House. This building, completed in 1774, houses exhibits of flags and paintings. A film depicting Cape Cod's history is presented. Visitors are welcome on weekday afternoons from 1:30 to 4:30. 6A is very busy here and very narrow. There is a sidewalk on the left and we recommend its use where there are no pedestrians.

About two miles from the start of the ride you'll pass the post office in the tiny community of Cummaquid. Turn left on Keveney Lane and head toward Mill Creek and Hallets' Mill Pond going downhill. When you cross the bridge you enter a corner of Yarmouthport, and Keveney Lane becomes Mill Lane. The view of the marsh and the impressive Anthony's Cummaquid Inn is absorbing. Water St. goes off to the left shortly after crossing the bridge. Continue on Mill Lane. Return to 6A and turn right heading back to Barnstable.

If you have time, when you get to Rte. 6 on Mill La., turn left and ride a half mile to Yarmouthport to the intersection with Strawberry La. on the right and Church St. on the left. Along this stretch are several attractions to visit briefly or to linger over. Three notable houses are open to the public which represents three hundred years of New England architecture: the Colonel John Thatcher House (1680), the Winslow Crocker House (1780), and the Captain Bangs Hallet House (1840). They are open to the public. The Botanical Trail of Yarmouthport commences at the Hallet House. The houses and Trail are

(Continued Page 26)

23

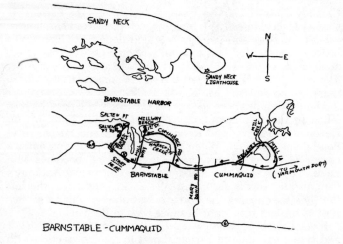

SANDY NECK

SANDY NECK LIGHTHOUSE

BARNSTABLE HARBOR

SALTEN PT

SALTEN PT RD

MILLWAY BEACH

COMMERCE RD

MARSH CREEK

START HERE

BARNSTABLE

MARY DUNN RD

CUMMAQUID

(TO YARMOUTH PORT)

N
W — E
S

BARNSTABLE - CUMMAQUID

**Directions for the ride:**

- Park at Sturgis Library or in the area.
- Head east on 6A.
- Turn left on Keveney La.
- Cross the bridge over Mill Creek.
- Head back to 6A on Mill La.
- Turn right on 6A.
- Turn right on Commerce Rd.
- Turn right on Mill Way and see the beach.
- Return to 6A on Mill Way.
- Turn right on 6A.
- Turn right on Rendezvous La. and go down to the water.
- Return on Rendezvous.
- Turn right on Salten Pt. Rd.
- Loop around on Salten Pt.
- Turn right on Rendezvous La. heading back to 6A.
- Turn left on 6A and return to the Sturgis Library and your car.

administered lovingly by the Historical Society of Old Yarmouthport.

After enjoying Yarmouthport turn around and head west again on Rte 6. Turn right on Commerce Rd. which circles a marsh and crosses Maraspin Creek. At Mill Way, turn right for a short ride to the parking lot at Blish Point overlooking Mill Way Beach and Barnstable Harbor—dotted with islands—sheltered by Sandy Neck across the way (which you may visit on the West Barnstable ride).

Retrace the route up Mill Way past the town docks to 6A. Turn right. Ride past the Sturgis Library (where your car is parked) then turn right on Rendezvous Lane for another short jaunt to the water. On the way down to, or back from, the end of Rendezvous Lane (which dead ends at the water providing a good picnic site), turn into Salten Point Rd. This road makes a loop and returns you to Rendezvous Lane. It offers some stunning glimpses of the harbor, as well as a closer look at the life style of some of Barnstable's burghers whose well appointed houses and lawns are on display around this circle. Return to 6A, turn left and head back to the Sturgis Library. Built in 1644, the Library's holdings include a Bible printed in 1603 as well as material relating to Cape Cod's history and geneology.

The Trayser Memorial Museum is also located in Barnstable on 6A. It was originally a Customs House. An old jail building is on the grounds. The collection is open to the public for a modest charge Tuesday through Saturday afternoons from 1:00 to 5:00.

# 5  Woods Hole - Falmouth

Number of miles: 26.5
Approximate pedalling time: 3 hours
Terrain: Varied—a lot of flat areas, other definitely hilly areas
Surface: Good
Things to see: Woods Hole Oceanographic Center, Woods Hole
  Aquarium, views of Buzzard's Bay and Vineyard Sound,
  Falmouth Historical Society Museum, Nobska Point
  Lighthouse.
How to get there: Head south from the Bourne Bridge on Rte.
  28A to West Falmouth. Park south of the intersection of Rte.
  28A and Brick Kiln Rd. in the parking lot of a tiny shopping
  center.


Ride south on 28-A. At Homestead Rd. turn left to see the
fieldstone and oak home built in 1678 by the Quaker Bowerman
family and lived in by the family until 1966. It is now open to the
public. Return to 28A and bear right at the fork onto a very
pretty narrow county road called Sippewisset Rd. After coming
down a hill Sippewisset goes sharply right while Palmer Ave.
goes left. Go right on Sippewisset Rd. It changes its name to
Quisset Ave. and then to School St. It continues to be quite
hilly.

Turn right on Beccles Rd. for a brief loop which returns you to
Sippewisset Rd. When you get to the crest of this hill, you'll see
an enormous frame inn on the bluffs.

Upon leaving the crest you'll be riding mainly downhill to
Woods Hole. At the first stop sign your route becomes Quisset
Ave. Ride up a long hill to the Woods Hole Golf Club which
overlooks Quisset Harbor. Your downhill run brings you
abruptly into the center of Woods Hole. Eel Pond is the
crowded anchorage to your right as you come into town; the
buildings bordering the pond are those of the three marine
research institutions: the National Marine Fisheries Service,
the Marine Biological Laboratory and the Woods Hole
Oceanographic Institute. Watch for the research vessels R/V
"ALBATROSS" and R/V "DOLPHIN," and visit the Woods
Hole Aquarium which is run by the National Marine Fisheries
Service and is free. Quisset Ave.—now School St.—"Ts" into
Water St. Go right on Water St. to the research facilities and to
(Continued Page 30)

27

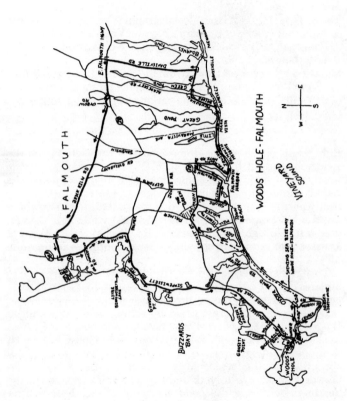

**Directions for the ride:**

- Start from the parking lot of a small shopping center on the right side of Rte. 28A just south of Brick Kiln Rd.
- Turn right (south) on Rte. 28A to Sippewisset Rd.
- Bear right on Sippewisset Rd. to Woods Hole. It will change its name to Quisset Ave. and then to School St. at Water St.
- Turn right on Water St. over the drawbridge, around the research facilities and back to Water St.
- Turn left on Water St. to Church St.
- Turn right on Church St. to Nobska Point and Nobska Lighthouse to Nobska Rd.
- Bear around to the left on Nobska Rd. to Oyster Pond Rd.
- Turn left on Oyster Pond to Woods Hole Rd.
- Bear left on Woods Hole Rd. to the Woods Hole Steamship Authority Parking lot.
- Go left across the bridge and down, circling to the right, a 180° turn into the parking lot.
- Go through the parking lot, on its left side, under the bridge, to the beginning of the Bike Path.
- Take the Shining Sea Bike Way to Falmouth, arriving on Woods Hole Rd.
- Bear right on Woods Hole Rd. to West Main St.
- Bear right on West Main St. to Shore St.
- Turn right on Shore St. to the Town Beach.
- Return via Shore St. to Clinton St.
- Turn right on Clinton to Scranton Ave.
- Turn left on Scranton to Robbins Rd.
- Turn right on Robbins Rd. to Falmouth Heights Rd.
- Turn right on Falmouth Heights Rd. to Irving St.
- Turn left on Irving St. and continue as it turns into Menauhant Rd.
- Bear left on Menauhant at the fork with Ocean Ave.
- Continue on Menauhant and bear right, cross Acapesket Rd. over the bridge to Davisville Rd.
- Turn left on Davisville Rd. to East Falmouth Hgwy.
- Turn left on East Falmouth Hgwy. to Ox Box Rd.
- Turn right on Ox Bow Rd. and curve around to the left and then right on Brick Kiln Rd. to Rte. 28A.
- Turn left on Rte. 28A and return to your starting place.

see the Candle House. A unique ship's bow sticks out of the front of the building.

To continue your route, take a loop to Nobska Point and back by heading east uphill (away from downtown Woods Hole) on Water St. past the ferry landing, and past the cove, turning right on Church St. From the Point the view of Vineyard Sound and the shoreline is superb. Enjoy picnicking and swimming at the Point. Now bear on around the point on what is now Nobska Rd. Ride under the Bicycle Trail then turn immediately left and go sharply uphill on Oyster Pond Rd. Continue bearing left and return to town. Head for the Woods Hole Steamship Authority parking lot. Turn at the sign ALL CARS FOR BOATS TURN HERE. Cross the parking lot in front of the Steamship Authority and enter the parking lot through the pedestrian entrance. Ride through the parking lot and go under the underpass.

You are now on the three and one-third mile long Shining Sea Bikeway connecting Woods Hole and downtown Falmouth, paralleling Fay Rd. along Vineyard Sound.

You'll emerge from the dramatic bikeway onto Woods Hole Rd. Bear right. At the fork bear right again onto W. Main St. by the Falmouth green. Watch for the elegant 1790 colonial on the green which is the Falmouth Historical Society Museum.

At Shore St. turn right and go down to the water, see the Town Beach, then go back up Shore two blocks to Clinton and turn right. Ride about eight blocks to Scranton Ave. on the Falmouth Inner Harbor. Skirt this beautiful, active harbor by going left on Scranton, right on Robbins Rd. at the top of the harbor and right on Falmouth Heights Rd. to go down the east side. This is another site from which you can ferry to Martha's Vineyard.

Bear right at the fork with Grand Ave., staying on Falmouth Heights Rd. until it "Ts" into Irving St. Go left and head uphill. Continue along this road, which becomes Menauhant Rd., passing Little Pond and Great Pond. At the fork with Ocean Ave. turn left and go inland staying on Menauhant Rd. At its intersection with Emerson (on the left), bear right, staying on Menauhant. Cross Acapesket Rd. then cross the bridge over Green Pond then turn left on Davisville Rd.

Turn left on East Falmouth Highway. In about three quarters of a mile cross the Coonamesett River and turn right on Ox Bow Rd. Curve around uphill and turn right going uphill on Brick Kiln Rd. Follow Brick Kiln to Rte. 28. Cross the Rte. 28-A and turn left to return to the shopping center parking lot.

# 6  Osterville - Centerville

Number of miles: 14
Approximate pedalling time: 1-½ hours
Terrain: Hilly
Surface: Good
Things to see: Towns of Osterville and Centerville, East, West
    and Great Bays, Crosby Ship Yard.
How to get there: From the intersection of Rtes. 149 and 28,
    head east toward Hyannis on Rte. 28. Take South County Rd.
    to the right. It becomes Main St. and delivers you to the
    center of Osterville.

Begin this ride in the village of Osterville. Park on Main St.
Mount up and do a loop around this lovely village by riding
downhill on Main St. (following the sign to HYANNIS). When
you get to the A&P take a right uphill onto West Bay Rd. Turn
right again on Wianno Ave. going past the post office and the
library. Return to Main St.

After the loop, you're back on top of the hill. Now bear left in
front of the Osterville Baptist Church, then go right following
the sign which reads FALMOUTH - 17 MILES. At the fire
station turn right on Pond Rd. You may use the sidewalk along
Pond Rd. Turn right on Bumps River Rd. You'll encounter some
uphills along here and then a nice downhill to a pond. At the fork
bear right onto N. Main St. The sign says TO CENTERVILLE.
At the "T" turn left remaining on N. Main St. Then, at the stop
sign turn right onto Main St. in Centerville. Now you're in for a
treat as Centerville's Main St. is exceptional. There are stately
old houses on both sides of the street, a handsome church, and
the 1856 Country Store which is full of handmade crafts and
gadgets to nourish your curiosity and pleasure. (Note: this short
stretch of road is shared with the Hyannis-Craigville ride. You
could, therefore, combine the two rides into a "figure eight"
ride of 19.5 miles.)

When Main St. intersects with S. Main St. there's a traffic
light. Turn right following the sign to OSTERVILLE. Proceed
on S. Main St. Now enjoy the views of East Bay. Turn left onto
East Bay Rd. following it to the "T" intersection with Wianno
Ave. Turn left onto Wianno and ride to Dowses Beach. Wianno
Ave. "Ts" into Sea View Ave. Turn right and follow Sea View to

(Continued Page 34)

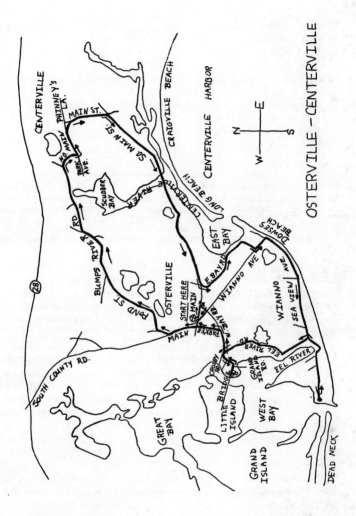

OSTERVILLE - CENTERVILLE

**Directions for the ride:**

- Park on Main St. in Osterville.
- Loop around the town's center by taking Main south east to W. Bay Rd.
- Turn right on W. Bay Rd.
- Turn right on Wianno Ave.
- Bear left in front of Osterville Baptist Church, going north.
- Turn right on Pond Rd.
- Turn right on Bumps River Rd.
- Bear right at the fork onto N. Main St.
- Turn left at the "T," remaining on N. Main St.
- Turn right onto Main St. at the stop sign.
- Turn right on S. Main St. at the traffic light.
- Turn left on E. Bay Rd.
- Turn left onto Wianno Ave. at the "T."
- Turn right onto Sea View Ave.
- Go to the end of Sea View Ave.
- Turn around and head back.
- Turn left on Eel River Rd.
- Turn left on W. Bay Rd.
- Go into Crosby's Boatyard.
- Turn right onto Grand Island Rd. upon leaving Crosby's.
- Turn right onto Bridge St.
- Return via Bridge and Grand Island to W. Bay Rd.
- Turn right on W. Bay Rd.
- Turn left onto Parker Rd. which becomes Main St., Osterville, and leads you to your car.

its end. After passing the gatehouses, backyards and driveways of the rich, and after experiencing an occasional open-mouthed stare at a house which would be more comfortable on a back lot at Warner Brothers than here facing the restless oceans and inlets of the Cape, you'll arrive at the end of Sea View Ave. Here you'll be overlooking a bar called Dead Neck, Grand Island and West Bay.

After enjoying the scene, retrace your route to just past Eel River and turn left on Eel River Rd. It will "T" into West Bay Rd. Turn left. Immediately you'll be at the Crosby Boatyard. Operational since 1840, this yard was the home of the Crosby Cat, the original Catboat. The Crosby Boatyard still handcrafts pleasure boats and provides marina services to boaters.

Leaving Crosby's turn right onto Grand Island Rd., then onto Bridge St. which crosses over to Little Island. From Little Island you may go by causeway to Grand Island which is an incorporated private preserve. Unless you are house-hunting, and so present yourself to the real estate office at the gatehouse where the troll keeps guard, you will not be welcome at Grand Island. Return to West Bay Rd. via Crosby's, then turn left on Parker Rd.—which turns into Main St.—and return to the village of Osterville.

# 7 Hyannis - Craigville

**Number of miles:** 15.5
**Approximate pedalling time:** 2 hours
**Terrain:** Varied
**Surface:** Good
**Things to see:** 1856 Country Store, Craigville Beach, Hyannis Harbor, Kalmus Beach Park, Sunset Hill, Kennedy Memorial.
**How to get there:** From Rte. 6 (Mid-Cape Hgwy.) take Rte. 132 south toward Hyannis; turn right on Barnstable Rd. and right again on Main St. Park in the Stop'n Shop parking lot on the corner of Main and High School Sts.

Ride west on Main St. which is one-way west. Enjoy Hyannis's unusual shops (e.g., the Scrimshaw Shop) then turn left on Sea St. heading for the waterfront. At the fork with Ocean Ave. bear right. When Ocean "Ts" into Hyannis Ave. turn left. Go right, uphill, on Washington to Craigville Beach Rd. Turn left. Promptly at the corner of Irving Ave. turn right and go to the top of what is called Sunset Hill. From here the view is panoramic. One can see Hyannis Harbor and the town to the left; and, to the right, Squaw Island, a magnificent marsh fed by the sea and Hall Creek, and Centerville Harbor. Because of the lay of the land—if your timing is right and you're there at sunset—you will see the sun drop astonishingly into the sea. Explore this lovely point further (if you can—this is Kennedy country!) then return to Craigville Beach Rd. and go uphill and inland. At the fork bear left, following the arrow to Craigville Beach. At the next stop sign, where Smith St. comes in from your right, continue straight ahead. The residential streets to your left frequently dead end but can be conveniently explored by bicycle and some offer new glimpses of the marsh.

Soon after passing Seventh Ave. you enter the community of Centerville. Here the streets on the left run down to Covell Beach. You'll soon arrive at crescent shaped Craigville Beach. This beach, together with Covell Beach and Downs Beach form the beaches of Centerville Harbor. These are lovely, clean beaches open to the public and run by the Township of Barnstable. By all means enjoy a swim here. (If you'd rather swim

(Continued Page 38)

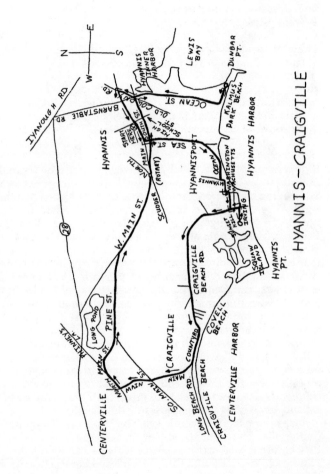

HYANNIS — CRAIGVILLE

**Directions for the ride:**

- Start the ride on the corner of Main and High School Sts.
- Go west on Main St. to Sea St.
- Turn left on Sea St. to Ocean Ave.
- Bear right onto Ocean Ave. to Hyannis Ave.
- Turn left on Hyannis to Washington St.
- Turn right on Washington to Craigville Beach Rd.
- Turn left on Craigville Beach Rd. to Irving Ave.
- Turn right on Irving Ave. to Sunset Hill.
- Turn around and return to Craigville Beach Rd.
- Turn left on Craigville Beach Rd. to County Rd.
- Turn right on County Rd. to Main St.
- Turn right on Main St.
- Cross S. Main and continue straight. Main St. changes to N. Main St.
- Bear right at the fork with Phinney's La. staying on N. Main. N. Main becomes Pine St. at its junction with S. Main St. Go to the rotary.
- Take the second right off the rotary which is still Main St. to South St.
- Bear right on South St. to Ocean St.
- Turn right on Ocean St. to Hyannis Harbor and the Kennedy Memorial and Kalmus Beach.
- Return from Kalmus Beach on Ocean St. to South St.
- Cross South St. onto old Colony Rd. to Main St.
- Turn left on Main St. to the corner of High School St. and your car.

closer to the end of the ride, another good beach on the route is Kalmus Park Beach in Hyannis.)

When you leave the beach you'll see that County Rd. forks with Long Beach Rd. which extends west along the shore. Continue north on Main St. following the signs to CENTER-VILLE - OSTERVILLE. At the traffic light, cross S. Main St. Continue straight ahead on what is now Main St. and enter the village of Centerville, passing the 1856 County Store on your right. On this remarkable street you'll pass one stately house after the next, including the Mary Lincoln house (1840), now a museum of the Centerville Historical Society.

Main St. continues north, then east. When it turns it is called N. Main St. Shortly after you start downhill on N. Main, watch for a stand of pine. Immediately before the trees N. Main bears off sharply to the right while Phinney's La. goes straight ahead; stay on N. Main. Pass Long Pond on the left. S. Main St. soon comes in from your right at which point the street becomes Pine St. It remains Pine until it merges with W. Main St. in Hyannis. Now there's a stretch of urban sprawl and you must do time zipping past Hyannis's fair share of supermarkets and hamburger stands.

At the traffic rotary pass Scudder and take the second street off the rotary which continues to be Main St. At the fork, you've arrived again in Hyannis Center whose main drags are one way. Bear right onto South St. In about six blocks, on the corner of Pearl St., your eye will be delighted and challenged by an octagonal house—painted pink! This private house was built in 1850 and is one of only a handful of such buildings in all of New England.

Turn right at the small park onto Ocean St. and drive down to the busy Hyannis Inner Harbor, where you can see commercial and pleasure boats, catch a cruise ship to Martha's Vineyard and Nantucket, enjoy a seafood dinner, catch your own seafood, or perhaps stay overnight at the Harborside Motel. After a stroll in this neighborhood, continue on Ocean St. to the Town Park on your left to see the Kennedy Memorial, if you like, or proceed a few blocks to the end of the street and you'll arrive at Kalmus Beach Park. Here one side of the beach is on the ocean and one side faces Lewis Bay. You may swim and picnic here.

Retrace your route up Ocean St. At the little park you will be faked out by Hyannis's one way streets. Turn right then bear straight across South St. onto Old Colony Rd. Take a left at the next corner onto Main St. and return four blocks to your car on the corner of Main and High School Sts.

# 8 West Yarmouth - South Yarmouth

Number of miles: 14.5
Approximate pedalling time: 2 hours
Terrain: Moderately hilly
Surface: Good
Things to see: Aqua Circus, Judah Baker Windmill, Yarmouth Herring Run.
How to get there: From the west take U.S. 6 to Rte. 132, 132 South to 28, and 28 East to West Yarmouth, to Berry Ave. The Yarmouth Police Station is on the northwest corner.

Start this ride by parking your car in the parking lot of the Home Federal Savings Bank on the southeast corner of Rte. 28 (Main St.) and Berry Ave. Proceed north on Berry Ave. A sign will point to ROUTE 6. Go through the typical Cape Cod pine forest here, uphill for eight tenths of a mile to the juncture with Buck Island Rd.; turn right. This is a well paved, two lane road which goes by cranberry bogs, off to the right. Come to West Yarmouth Rd. Turn left on this two lane road. Pass through patches of open countryside, still climbing, as you go inland from the shore. Three miles into the ride you come to Old Town House Rd.; turn right. There is a country feeling out here, where the land is sparsely settled. Old Town House Rd. is a big three lane road, still going uphill. In one and a quarter miles turn right on Station Ave., a gently rolling road, which goes mostly downhill.

Just past the Regional High School on your left, across from the football field, turn right onto the unmarked road that is Long Pond Dr. Skirt Long Pond which you can glimpse through the trees to your left. At the end of Long Pond, after passing Winslow Gray Rd. on the right, turn left on Mercury Drive. At the point where Venus Rd. comes in from the right and Mars La. also goes off at an angle to the right, continue straight ahead on Mercury Dr., which will "T" into Lymon La. Turn right on little Lyman La. and go down to Rte. 28, turn left and then immediately right onto Wood La. Go past a small, wooded lane divider where there's a statue of a fireman. Just past this spot, turn right onto Wood Rd., a narrow residential street. Cross

(Continued Page 42)

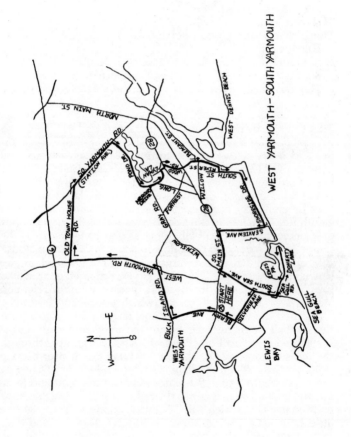

WEST YARMOUTH – SOUTH YARMOUTH

**Directions for the ride:**

- Start from the parking lot at the Home Federal Savings Bank on the S. E. corner of Rte. 28 (Main St.) and Berry Ave.
- Go north on Berry Ave. to Buck Island Rd.
- Turn right on Buck Island Rd. to West Yarmouth Rd. to Old Town House Rd.
- Turn right on Old Town House Rd. to Station Ave.
- Turn right on Station Ave. to Long Pond Dr.
- Turn right on Long Pond Dr. (may not be marked—across from the High School football field) to Mercury Dr.
- Turn left on Mercury Dr. and go straight, past Venus Rd. and Mars La. to Lyman La.
- Turn right on Lyman La. to Rte. 28.
- Turn left on Rte. 28 and immediately right onto Wood La. to Wood Rd.
- Turn right on Wood Rd., cross Main St. and go straight on what is now River St., to South St.
- Turn right on South St. to Shore Side Dr.
- Bear left on Shore Side Dr. to Seaview Ave.
- Turn left on Seaview Ave. to the point on the shore.
- Return up Seaview Ave. to Main St.
- Turn left on Main St. to South Sea Ave.
- Turn left on South Sea Ave. to Sea Gull Rd.
- Turn left on Sea Gull Rd. to Doherty Rd. to Sea Gull Beach.
- Return via Doherty Rd. to Sea Gull Rd. to South Sea Ave.
- Turn right on the South Sea Ave. to Silver Leaf La.
- Turn left on Silver Leaf La. to Berry Ave.
- Turn right on Berry to S. Main St. and your starting place.

Main St. (Rte. 28) and the road you're on is now called River St., which takes you down to and briefly along the Bass River.

At the fork with Pleasant St., bear right on River St. Soon after the fork, come to a Judah Baker Windmill on the bank of the Bass River in tiny Windmill Park. There's a nice little beach here. The Windmill was originally built in 1791 in South Dennis and moved here in 1863. The town now owns it and is restoring it. It should be open by the summer of 1977. Continue on River St. which swings around 90° to the right and then comes to South St. where there's a stop sign. Turn left onto South St. which takes you down to Shore Side Dr. Run Pond is on your right. The Bass River Beach is here on the curve just as you get to the shore line. There are lots of motels, cottages, and quiet houses. You are now on Shore Side Drive. Proceed along the waterfront. There are houses between you and the water but you can go down any one of the streets running off to your left to the shore. There are several public beaches along this road. At the stop sign with Seaview Ave., turn left past the Beach House Motor Lodge to the point, a nice place to take a break and get a great, unimpeded view of the ocean. Turn around and go straight up Seaview Ave. to Main St., on Rte. 28. There's a stop sign. Turn left. The Aqua Circus is on the right. They have six shows a day, featuring dolphins. Stop and take a look. Just past the Aqua Circus comes South Sea Ave. and a traffic light where you turn left and return to the shore line.

Sea Gull Rd. comes up in a mile, turn left onto it, and head for Sea Gull Beach. Lewis Pond will be in sight to your left. Stretches of the road become a causeway across the marshes. Beautiful Sea Gull Beach is open from 8:00 a.m. to 10:00 p.m. There are restroom facilities. After your swim and/or picnic, return to South Sea Ave. via Sea Gull Rd. Turn right on South Sea and then, about four blocks up, turn left onto Silver Leaf Lane which will take you five eighths of a mile to Berry Ave. There is a stop sign but no street sign; however, you'll be able to identify it because Silver Leaf Lane jogs to the left after it crosses Berry. Turn right on Berry which will take you back up to S. Main St. where you started your ride.

# 9   West Dennis - Harwichport

Number of miles: 15.8
Approximate pedalling time: 2 hours
Terrain: Flat to moderately hilly
Surface: Good
Things to see: Towns of Harwich and Harwichport, Allen
   Harbor, Glendon Beach, Swan River, West Dennis Beach.
How to get there: From the west take Rte. 6 to Rte. 134 in South
   Dennis. Take 134 south to Rte. 28, turn right onto Rte. 28 and
   proceed three eighths of a mile to the intersection of Rte. 28
   and Trotting Park Rd.

Start this ride in the parking lot of the Ezra H. Baker Public
School on the corner of Rte. 28 and Trotting Park Rd.

Head north on Trotting Park Rd. A stop sign comes up shortly
at the intersection with Centre St. There is a little triangular
shaped park here and the substantial Congregational Church of
South Dennis can be seen on the right after crossing over
Centre St. Continue north on what is now old Main St. There
are many handsome houses out this way. About one mile from
the church there is a fork where there is a little stone marker in a
tiny park. Main St. goes to the left. Go right on what is Duck
Pond Rd. (although there is no street sign for it).

In two fifths of a mile there is a traffic light at Rte. 134. Cross
134 onto Upper County Rd. and then immediately turn left onto
Great Western Rd. Bear around at the "Y" and head east on
Great Western. About one and a quarter miles from this point
enter the township of Harwich. Soon you will pass Depot Rd.
and then Bell's Neck Rd., starting a gradual downhill past Sand
Pond on the left, and a reservoir on the right. This mid-Cape
area is rolling, and in some stretches, steeply hilly.

When you approach the little town of Harwich, Great Western Rd. becomes Main St. Harwich is complete and lovely with
its Congregational Church and a sprinkling of antique shops on
its attractive Main St. At the intersection of Rte. 124 pass the
Congregational Church on Main St. If you turn right briefly on
Rte. 124 (Sisson Rd.) you will see the Brooks Academy which is
now the Harwich Historical Society Museum. It is an interesting place to visit but it is only open on Monday, Wednesday and
Friday from 1:30 to 4:30 p.m.

(Continued Page 46)

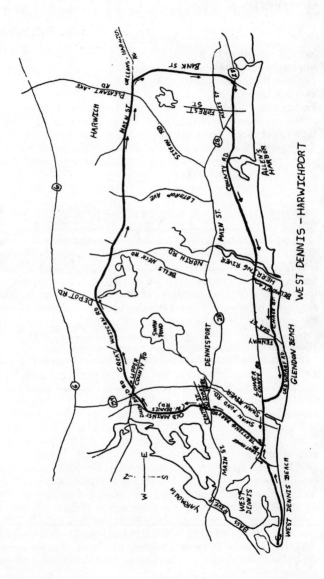

WEST DENNIS - HARWICHPORT

**Directions for the ride:**

- Start from the parking lot of the Ezra H. Baker Public School at the corner of Rte. 28 and Trotting Park Rd.
- Turn north on Trotting Park Rd. to Centre St.
- Cross Centre St. and continue north on what is now called Old Main St. to Duck Pond Rd.
- Bear right on Duck Pond Rd. to Rte. 134.
- Cross Rte. 134 onto Upper County Rd. to Great Western Rd.
- Turn left on Great Western Rd. to Harwichtown where Great Western Rd. becomes Main St.
- Continue on Main St. to Bank St.
- Turn right on Bank St. to Rte. 28.
- Turn right on Rte. 28 to County Rd.
- Bear left on County Rd. to Belmont Rd.
- Turn left on Belmont Rd. to Chase Ave.
- Turn right on Chase Ave. to Old Wharf Rd.
- Turn left on Old Wharf Rd. to Lower County Rd.
- Turn left on Lower County Rd. to Lighthouse Rd.
- Turn left on Lighthouse to the West Dennis Public Beach.
- Return up Lighthouse Rd. to Lower County Rd.
- Turn right on Lower County Rd. to Trotting Park Rd.
- Turn left on Trotting Park Rd. to Rte. 28 and your starting place.

Riding along on Main St. watch for Bank St. as you enjoy Harwich, which is a picturesque village with old houses and a pleasant air.

Leaving Harwich on Bank St. there is a good downhill run to Harwichport past cranberry bogs here and there, for a nice one and a half mile ride. At the junction of Rte. 28 and Bank St. turn right and ride west on 28 until the fork where Rte. 28 goes off to the right and County Rd. bears left. (If you have time, take a detour down to Wychmere Harbor by turning left when Bank St. "Ts" into Rte. 28 and going east for about a quarter of a mile to Wychmere Rd. Turn right. Enjoy your visit to this scenic harbor, then return to Rte. 28, head west, and continue the bike trail.) You take County Rd.

Ride through Harwichport with its interesting old houses, churches and little shops. Continue past Allen's Harbor, a tiny protected habor right off the road, and over the Herring River into Dennisport where you'll see some of the southernmost part of that town. There is a lovely view of the harbor, the docks, and the windmill out on the point. This is a nice place to stop and enjoy yourself.

Turn left on Belmont Rd. and at the end of it turn right on Chase Ave. where the road parallels Motel Mecca. Follow closely when it goes right and then turn immediately left onto Old Wharf Rd. At the five way intersection, cross Sea St. and continue straight ahead on Old Wharf Rd. and you'll come upon Glendon Beach which is public. Old Wharf Rd. ends at the stop sign at Lower County Rd.; turn left.

Shortly afterwards cross over the Swan River with its fascinating marsh lands. Turn left onto Lighthouse Rd. There will be a sign to the Town Beach right across from a marsh; continue down to the extensive and beautiful West Dennis Public Beach.

When you're ready to go, return up Lighthouse Rd. to Lower County Rd. and turn right. Ride as far as Trotting Park Rd.; turn left. Ride the one mile back to your starting place at Rte. 28 and Trotting Park Rd.

# 10  Harwich - West Chatham

Number of miles: 14.1
Approximate pedalling time: 2 hours
Terrain: Rolling hills
Surface: Good
Things to see: Town of Harwich, Brooks Free Library, Town
   Beach, Cockle Cove, Ridgevale Beach, central Cape Cod
   countryside.
How to get there: From the west take Rte. 6 to Rte. 124 in the
   township of Harwich. Go right on 124 to the center of
   Harwich.

Start your ride in the center of Harwich, on Main St., near the
juncture of Rtes. 39 and 124.
   Harwich is a lovely, small, New England town with its grace-
ful white Congregational Church. It has some five antique
shops on its Main St. Great for browsing. If you have pannier
bags you might find that small gee-gaw you've looked every-
where for.
   Ride east on Main St., past the Brooks Free Library. You
might stop in here to see the collection of 19th Century statuary
by John Roger. They are set in a Victorian atmosphere. Then
you pass the band stand and ball field, to a "Y" where you will
bear right on Chatham Rd. Main St. is lined with trees that are
larger and taller than those found closer to the sea. One and a
half miles down Chatham Rd., you'll come to a "T" intersection
with Rte. 28. Turn right onto 28 and ride a short distance to
Deep Hole Rd.; turn left and ride a half mile down to the small
but lovely town beach. There are rest rooms here. When you're
ready to leave, take the road that starts just across from the rest
rooms. This is Uncle Venies Rd. although it may not be so
marked.
   Ride up one quarter mile and turn right onto S. Chatham Rd.
The route is parallel to the beach and ocean here, and providing
a fine view across the salt marsh. Pass Soundview coming in
from the left. Once you pass over into Chatham this road
becomes Deep Hole Rd., although there might not be a sign.
Go uphill for a short distance, then the road levels off just before
the "T" intersection with Pleasant St. There's a stop sign here.
Turn left onto Pleasant St. and ride up to Rte. 28. Turn right
onto 28. There's a village store and snack bar on the corner. This

(Continued Page 50)

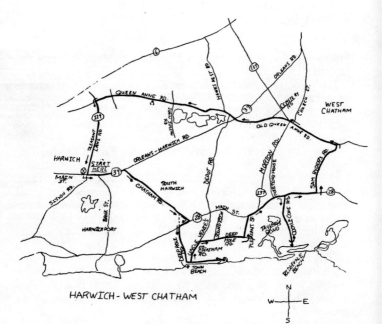

HARWICH - WEST CHATHAM

**Directions for the ride:**

- Start on Main St. in Harwich, near the junction of Rtes. 39 and 124.
- Go east on Main St. to Chatham Rd.
- Bear right on Chatham Rd. to Rte. 28.
- Turn right on Rte. 28 to Deep Hole Rd.
- Turn left on Deep Hole Rd. to the Town Beach.
- Return from the beach up Uncle Venies Rd. to S. Chatham Rd.
- Turn right on S. Chatham Rd., which becomes Deep Hole Rd., to Pleasant St.
- Turn left on Pleasant St. to Rte. 28.
- Turn right on Rte. 28 to Cockle Cove Rd.
- Turn right on Cockle Cove Rd. to the beach.
- Return up Cockle Cove Rd. to Rte. 28.
- Turn right on Rte. 28 to Sam Ryders Rd.
- Turn left on Sam Ryders Rd. to Queen Anne Rd.
- Turn left on Queen Anne Rd. to Rte. 124.
- Turn left on Rte. 124 to Main St. in Harwich.
- Turn onto Main St. to go to your starting place.

is a rolling road. Follow it for three quarters of a mile, past Rte. 137 which comes in from the left, to Cockle Cove Rd. There's a sign saying COCKLE COVE; turn right and go down to the cove and Ridgevale Beach which you get to by crossing a small foot bridge.

After visiting the beach, retrace the route back up the same road to Rte. 28, where you turn right and then left on Sam Ryders Rd. It's mostly uphill here for almost one mile to a "T" intersection with Queen Anne Rd. Turn left here. Stay on Queen Anne Rd. for four miles now, to the intersection with Rte. 124. Note that Queen Anne Rd. is not well marked so follow the map and instructions carefully. Pass Church St. and then cross Rte. 137 which bends here and is called Morton Rd. on your left and Long Pond on your right. Continue straight and soon Cemetery Rd. will come in from your right and merge into Queen Anne Rd. Stay on Queen Anne. You'll come to a stop sign on Rte. 39 which you cross over and continue past a small pond, then Bucks Pond and Josephs Pond, all on your left. Just past the ponds, the road widens. At the intersection of Queen Anne Rd. and Rte. 124, there is a stop sign. Turn left onto Rte. 124, which is called Pleasant Lake Rd. From here the route is mostly downhill for one mile to Harwich, and your starting place.

# 11  West Brewster - Dennis

Number of miles: 21
Approximate pedalling time: 3 hours
Terrain: Hilly
Surface: Good to excellent
Things to see: Stony Brook Grist Mill, Chapin Memorial Beach, New England Fire and History Museum, Sesuit Neck Harbor, Sealand, The Drummer Boy Museum, Museum of Natural History and Smock Windmill, Joshea Dennis Manse. .
How to get there: From the west take Rte. 6A just into Brewster and watch for the New England Fire and History Museum on the left, just before the Town Hall. From the east take 6A through Brewster past the intersection of Rtes. 124 and 137 to the Museum.


Begin this ride on Rte. 6A just west of Rte. 137 (Long Pond Rd.). Park in the lot of the New England Fire and History Museum. Come out of the parking lot and turn right onto Main St. (Rte. 6A). At the fork where 6A goes right, take the left hand, which is Stony Brook Rd. There's also a sign indicating a Bike Route in this direction. You'll pass Smith Pond on the left and then a series of ponds.

You'll soon begin a stiff uphill and then take a steep downhill. About three quarters of a mile from the fork you'll come upon the Stony Brook Mill on the left. This grist mill still works to show you how it was done. It is open from 2:00-5:00 p.m. Wednesdays, Fridays and Saturdays in July and August.

There's a fork just beyond the mill; here, bear left onto Setucket Rd. This road is hilly. You pass a lovely placid little pond and go through a forested area. Two miles from the fork of Setucket and Stony Brook Rds. there is another pond where you bear right, remaining on Setucket Rd. There is much open, unsettled country through here, very much like parts of Connecticut. In another mile cross Rte. 134., then cross River Rd. Setucket becomes a roller coaster, winding around and rolling up and down. You'll be able to see Follins Pond to the left from the ridge. At the crest of a hill, at the intersection of Setucket, North Dennis, and South Yarmouth Rds. turn right onto South Yarmouth Rd. Here there are some downhill runs as you head back to Rte. 6A, just about a mile away. Arriving at 6A, turn

(Continued Page 54)

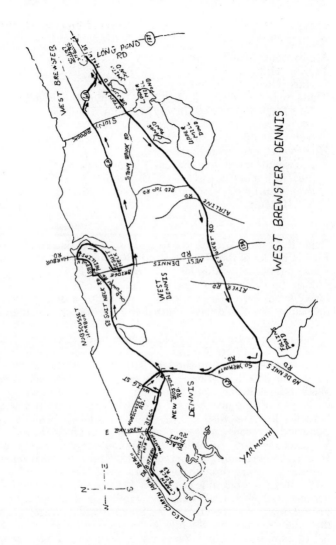

WEST BREWSTER - DENNIS

**Directions for the ride:**

- Start in the parking lot of the New England Fire and History Museum on Rte. 6A just west of Rte. 137 in Brewster.
- Go right on Main St. (Rte. 6A) to Stony Brook Rd.
- Turn left on Stony Brook Rd. to Setucket Rd.
- Turn left on Setucket Rd. to So. Yarmouth Rd.
- Turn right on So. Yarmouth Rd. to Rte. 6A.
- Turn right on Rte. 6A to New Boston Rd.
- Turn left on New Boston Rd. to Beach St.
- Bear right on Beach St. to Taunton Ave.
- Bear left on Taunton Ave. which becomes Dr. Bottero Rd. and then Chapin Beach Rd. to Chapin Beach.
- Return via Chapin Beach Rd., Bottero Rd., Taunton Ave. and Beach St. to Whig St.
- Turn left on Whig St. to Nobscusset Rd.
- Turn right on Nobscusset Rd. to Rte. 6A.
- Turn left on Rte. 6A to Sesuit Neck Rd.
- Bear left on Sesuit Neck Rd. to Old Town La.
- Bear left on Old Town La. to Bridge St.
- Turn left on Bridge St. to Stephen Phillips Rd.
- Bear left then right onto Stephen Phillips Rd. which becomes Harbor Rd.
- Go right on Harbor Rd. which becomes Sesuit Neck Rd. to Bridge St.
- Turn left on Bridge St. to Rte. 6A.
- Turn left on Rte. 6A to your starting place in Brewster.

right and go three-fourths of a mile to New Boston Rd. on the left. Take a hairpin turn to the left onto New Boston Rd. which is just across from the Dennis Public Market. Almost immediately there is a fork with Beach St.; bear right onto Beach. Easy Bay View comes in from the right; go left heading for Chapin Beach on Taunton Ave. It's a three way fork; take the one furthest left. Taunton soon turns into Dr. Bottero Rd. at a sharp left. This is a dune and grass area with water on both sides, now called Chapin Beach Rd. at the George Halliday Chapin Memorial Beach. Continue out through the dunes—great for sun bathing, getting lost in, or what have you. Follow the paved road as far as it goes and you come to Chapin Beach. Return the same way, via Dr. Bottero Rd., Taunton Ave. and Beach St. Stay on Beach as far as Whig St. on the left. It's the next street after Tory La., of course. Turn left onto Whig St. Go to the next intersection which is with Nobscusset Rd. and turn right. At this corner is the Joshea Dennis Manse, a grey shingled house, built in 1736 for the Rev. Dennis (Manse means the residence of a minister).

Follow Nobscusset Rd. back to Rte. 6A then turn left and head east toward East Dennis and Brewster. Ride along 6A, using the sidewalk wherever possible, for slightly more than a mile to the fork where Sesuit Neck Rd. bears left. Ride along on it for one-half mile until Old Town La. comes in from the left at a fork with a little traffic island. "T" into Bridge St. shortly and turn left and then right onto Stephen Phillips Rd. and follow it as it turns left, down to the seashore and right on Harbor Rd. to Sesuit Neck Harbor. Continue around the busy little harbor on Harbor Rd. until it becomes Sesuit Neck Rd. Follow this to the intersection with Bridge St., where you turn left and go up to 6A. Turn left onto 6A and ride past the salt marshes into Brewster. There are several attractions along this section of the bike route: Sealand of Cape Cod is an extensive commercial aquarium. The Drummer Boy Museum is also a commercial venture. The museum has thirty acres of scenic countryside and picnic grounds. If you go there, visit the restored 18th Century Smock Windmill. The Museum of Natural History provides exhibits illustrating Cape Cod's ecology, a salt water aquarium and nature trails.

At the intersection where Stony Brook Rd. goes off to the right, go left. This road is now Main St. in Brewster as well as being Rte. 6A so you'll soon come to the start of the ride at the New England Fire History Museum.

# 12   Brewster

**No. of miles:** 16.0
**Approximate time:** 2½ hours
**Terrain:** Moderately hilly
**Surface:** Good
**Things to see:** Nickerson State Forest, Brewster, Brewster and
   Harwich countryside, Bassett's Animal Farm, Brewster
   General Store.
**How to get there:** Take Rte. 6A east to Brewster and the
   entrance to Nickerson State Forest. Coming down 6A from
   the east, you'll find the State Forest on your left about one
   and a half miles west of the junction of Rtes. 6 and 6A.

Start this ride in the parking lot of Nickerson State Park, just off
Rte. 6A in Brewster. Facing the park, a bike path starts on the
left, a short distance from the entrance. This paved path is just
for you and it winds its way mostly downhill for approximately
two miles through the park. When it first crosses the road bear
left and continue paralleling the road. Within a half mile Flax
Pond Rd. goes off to the left. Continue on past this road to the
intersection of Deer Park Rd., Nook Rd., and Joe Longs Rd.
There is a little grassy island in the middle and a sign announc-
ing that all campers must register before occupying campsites.
   Turn right, still on a bike path, and go downhill, parallel to
what is called Joe Long's Road. It is three tenths of a mile from
the intersection of the end of the bike path when Joe Long's Rd.
joins Millstone Rd. Turn left here. Ride on Millstone Rd. for
one and a half miles until it "Ts" into Rte. 137 which is also called
Long Pond Rd. Turn left and ride two and a half miles through a
forest where the colors are gorgeous in the fall, to the point, just
before Rte. 6, where Long Pond Rd. goes 90° right. Turn right
and ride through scrub pine forests on either side. There will be
an occasional glimpse of Long Pond on the right. When Long
Pond Rd. "Ts" into Rte. 124, turn right, and ride up 124 towards
Brewster. Pass between two lakes, Long Pond on the right, and
Seymour Pond on the left. Rte. 124, the Brewster-Harwich Rd.,
passes through a wooded area for three and a half miles. Pass the
Sweetwater Forest, a private campground, and one of the very
few open all year around, and Bassett's Animal Farm, about one
quarter mile off to the right. It's a delightful small zoo with hay

(Continued Page 58)

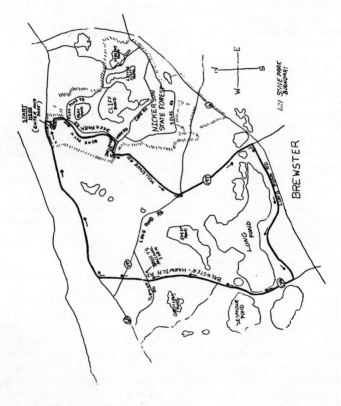

**Directions for the ride:**

- Start from the parking lot of Nickerson State Park, just off Rte. 6A in Brewster.
- Take the Bike Path that begins a short distance from the entrance, on your left facing into the park, and runs along Deer Park Rd.
- Go to the intersection of Deer Park, Nook and Joe Long's Rd.
- Turn right, on the bike path, and go along Joe Long's Rd. to Millstone Rd.
- Turn left on Millstone Rd. to Rte. 137 (Long Pond Rd.)
- Turn left on Rte. 137 to the junction where Rte. 137 and Long Pond Rd. separate.
- Turn right on Long Pond Rd. to Rte. 124.
- Turn right on Rte. 124 to Rte. 6A.
- Turn right on Rte. 6A to Nickerson State Park and your starting place.

rides and a petting menagerie. There is a modest admission fee. Just before you come to Rte. 6A cross Rte. 137 (Long Pond Rd.).

At Rte. 6A turn right and head back the three miles to the starting place at Nickerson State Park. But first, stop and visit the Brewster Store ("Groceries and General Merchandise") at the 124 intersection. This is an honest old-fashioned general store with a big pot bellied stove circled with benches. We've been here in the fall and the stove gave plenty of warmth—a rewarding stop on a brisk day.

# 13 Chatham

Number of miles: 21.5
Approximate pedalling time: 3 hours
Terrain: Hilly to flat
Surface: Good
Things to see: The beautiful town and harbors of Chatham,
    Chatham Fish Pier, Chatham Lighthouse.
How to get there: From the west take Rte. 28 directly into
    Chatham and proceed to the starting place in the center of
    Chatham.

Begin the ride in the parking lot of the shopping center at the
junction of Queen Anne Rd. and Rte 28 in Chatham. It's a five
point intersection. When you leave the parking lot bearing right
on Queen Anne's Rd., you'll be on a marked Bike Route. Pass
the First Church of Christ, Scientist on the left. At the "Y"
continue right on Pond St. (Queen Anne's Rd. goes up to the
left). Circle enormous Oyster Pond which has a public beach. At
the stop sign of the "T" intersection, turn right onto Stage
Harbor Rd. At the "Y" intersection with Cedar St. turn right
onto Cedar St. When Cedar St. "Ts" into Battlefield Rd., turn
left and ride along Battlefield until the "T" with Champlain Rd.
Turn left onto Champlain, still following the Bike Route. Very
soon Champlain makes a 90° bend to the left at the shore of
Stage Harbor. You can see Stage Harbor Lighthouse out there
as your route takes you along the shore of this beautiful harbor.
Look for the nun and can buoys marking the channel. There are
fishing boats at Old Mill Boatyard and Chatham Fisheries af-
fording an interesting scene.

Champlain Rd. turns left and becomes Stage Harbor Rd.
Bear left and shortly you will come to a stop sign where Bridge
St. is on the right; turn right onto it. There's a nice little dock
here. Go over the drawbridge and go straight until you come to a
"T" with Morris Island Rd. Turn right to go down Morris Island
Rd. On the left is the Chatham Lighthouse. When you come to
Little Beach Rd. straight ahead, you bear right, continuing on
Morris Island Rd. Bear left and down and across the causeway.
You're on Morris Island and when you come to the end of the
road there's a sign saying QUITNESSET. At this point the
Monomoy National Wildlife Refuge walking trail starts, so take

(Continued Page 62)

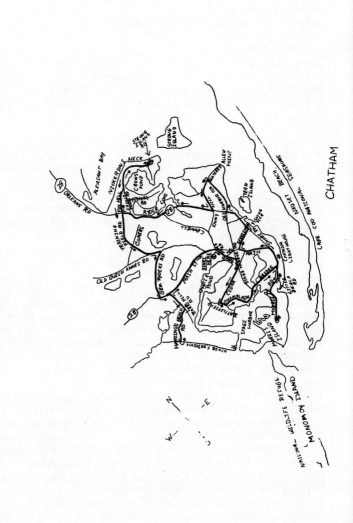

CHATHAM

**Directions for the ride:**

- Start from the shopping center parking lot at the junction of Queen Anne Rd. and Rte. 28 in Chatham.
- Go out and right on Queen Anne Rd. to Pond St.
- Bear right on Pond St. to Stage Harbor Rd.
- Turn right on Stage Harbor Rd. to Cedar St.
- Turn right on Cedar St. to Battlefield Rd.
- Turn left on Battlefield Rd. to Champlain Rd.
- Turn left on Champlain Rd., which goes 90° left and becomes Stage Harbor Rd., to Bridge St.
- Turn right on Bridge St. to Morris Island Rd.
- Turn right on Morris Island Rd. across the causeway to the turnaround.
- Return on Morris Island Rd. past Bridge St. and straight on Shore Rd. to Main St.
- Turn left on Main St. to Seaview St.
- Turn right on Seaview to Shore Rd.
- Turn left on Shore Rd. to Old Harbor Rd.
- Turn right on Old Harbor Rd. to Scatteree Rd.
- Turn left on Scatteree Rd. which goes left and becomes Stony Hill Rd. to Rte. 28.
- Turn right on Rte. 28 to Fox Hill Rd.
- Turn right on Fox Hill Rd. to Strong Island Rd.
- Turn left on Strong Island Rd. to the end.
- Return via Strong Island Rd. to Fox Hill Rd.
- Bear right on Fox Hill Rd. to Rte. 28 where Fox Hill crosses and becomes Training Field Rd. Continue straight on Training Field Rd. to where it merges with Old Queen Anne Rd.
- Bear left on Old Queen Anne Rd. to George Ryders Rd.
- Turn right on George Ryders Rd. to Rte. 28.
- Turn left on Rte. 28 to Barn Hill Rd.
- Turn right on Barn Hill Rd. to Hardings Beach Rd.
- Turn right on Hardings Beach Rd. to the beach.
- Return via Hardings Beach and Barn Hill Rds. to Rte. 28.
- Turn right on Rte. 28 and return to the starting place.

an exploring walk. When you're ready, double back across the dike. Stage Harbor is on the left. At the stop sign continue straight past the Chatham Lighthouse.

Take in the view, looking past Nauset Beach to the Atlantic Ocean. In a few blocks at Main St. turn left and go up past all the little shops—very picturesque—to the corner of Seaview and Main; turn right and go up a steep curve to the right which takes you to Shore Rd. Turn left. Ride one long block then turn sharply right at the sign TOWN OF CHATHAM FISH PIER. From this pier fishing boats go out all year round to supply us with fresh haddock, cod and scallops.

Go back to Shore Rd. and turn right. At the traffic light Old Harbor Rd. crosses Shore. Turn right onto it and go downhill here. At the "T" of Old Harbor and Scatteree Rds., turn left on Scatteree, again following the Bike Route. Bend around to the left, downhill past Old Mail Rd., on what is now called Stony Hill Rd. until you come to Rte. 28; turn right. It's downhill here. At a "Y" with Crow's Pond Rd., continue bearing left until you come to Fox Hill Rd. Turn right and follow Fox Hill Rd. up and out on Nickerson's Neck to the end of the public road. Take Strong Island Rd. to the left and go to the end, where it overlooks Strong Island. Across on the left is the mainland of Cape Cod. This whole area is protected by the long arm of Nauset Beach. Back track to Fox Hill then bear right and return with a view of Crow's Pond on the left as you ride. At the intersection of Crow's Hill and Fox Hill Rds. bear right on Fox Hill. At the stop sign intersection with Rte. 28, continue straight across on what is now called Training Field Rd. Cross Old Comers Rd. and soon come to Old Queen Ann Rd. which comes in from the right. Training Field Rd. merges with it. Continue, bearing to the left, on Old Queen Anne Rd.

When George Ryders Rd. comes in from the right, turn right onto it and follow it past the airport to Rte. 28 where you turn left and very shortly come to Barn Hill Rd. Turn right. This road goes downhill and curves left and right to a "Y" with Hardings Beach Rd. Turn right on Hardings Beach Rd. and follow it to the beach. This is a public beach with sand dunes. It extends for a mile to the left to Stage Harbor Lighthouse.

After spending some time at this beach, re-trace the route back to Rte. 28 where you turn right and head back into another two lane road, and your starting place.

# 14   Orleans

No. of miles: 13.2
Approximate pedalling time: 2 hours
Terrain: Moderately hilly
Surface: Good
Things to see: French Cable Museum, Town Cove, Nauset
  Harbor, Nauset Beach, Packet Landing, Rock Harbor, Inn of
  the Yankee Fisherman.
How to get there: From the south take 28 or 6A into Orleans and
  proceed to the Inn of the Yankee Fisherman just before the
  town line of Orleans and Eastham. Turn left into the
  shopping Center parking lot. On Rte. 6, proceed to the rotary
  just past the Orleans-Eastham town line and double back on
  6A and 28.


Start your ride in the Stop and Shop parking lot which is just
across from the Inn of the Yankee Fisherman on Rtes. 6A and
28, just before the Orleans-Eastham town line.
  Leave your bike carrier here and ride out to 6A and 28; turn
right. You quickly come to a "Y" intersection where 28 and 6A
split. Bear left on Rte. 28. In one third of a mile come to Cove
Rd.; turn left and go down the short hill to the shores of Town
Cove. The tiny Orleans Yacht Club is located here at the inner-
most end of this long cove which is bordered by Orleans and
Eastham. Come back up the short but steep hill. You will be
turning left here, but first take a look into the French Cable
Museum on the corner. The building housed the United States
terminus of the original Atlantic Cable and is now a museum,
open only Friday through Monday, 2:00-4:00 p.m. It is full of
fascinating old equipment.
  Now turn left onto 28 and almost immediately 45° left at a "Y"
to Main St. where you turn 90° left, on your way to Nauset
Beach. Another short ride brings you to the intersection of Main
St. and Tonset Rd. Turn left onto Tonset. Over on your left
there is a nice view of Town Cove. Continue on Tonset through
woods on the left and characteristic Cape Cod houses on the
right, past Gibson Rd. and Brick Hill Rd., straight out to the
dead end where Tonset Rd. overlooks Nauset Harbor, which is a
cut through Nauset Beach. This is three and a half miles from
your starting point.
  Turn around and go back up Tonset Rd. to Brick Hill Rd.; turn
(Continued Page 66)

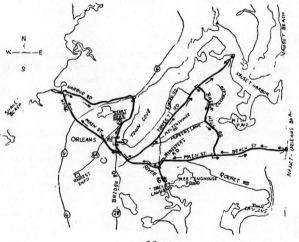

ORLEANS

**Directions for the ride:**

● Start from the parking lot of the shopping center, just across from the Inn of the Yankee Fisherman on Rtes. 6A and 28 in Orleans.
● Go out and turn right on 6A and 28 to the "Y" where 6A and 28 split.
● Bear left on Rte. 28 to Cove Rd.
● Turn left on Cove Rd. to the shore.
● Return up Cove Rd. to Rte. 28.
● Turn left on Rte. 28 to Main St.
● Turn left on Main St. to Tonset Rd.
● Turn left on Tonset Rd. to the dead end at Nauset Harbor.
● Return via Tonset Rd. to Brick Hill Rd.
● Turn left on Brick Hill Rd. to Beach Rd., a "T" intersection.
● Turn left on Beach Rd. to Nauset Beach.
● Return via Beach Rd. to Main St.
● Bear right on Main St. to Ministers Rd.
● Turn left on Minister's Rd. to River Rd.
● Bear left on River Rd. to Packet Landing.
● Return via River Rd., bearing left, to Main St.
● Turn left on Main St., cross 28 and 6A and continue on what is now Rock Harbor Rd. to Rock Harbor.
● Come back from the docks to Rock Harbor Rd.
● Turn left on Rock Harbor Rd. to the rotary of Rtes. 6, 6A and 28.
● Turn right, around the rotary, to the south towards Orleans on 6A and 28 to your starting place.

left. There should be a sign here directing you to Nauset Beach. Continue on Brick Hill as it twists and turns, passing Champlain and Hopkins La., passing through some wooded areas which are alive with color in the fall. About one and a half miles from your turn onto Brick Hill, there is a "T" intersection with Beach Rd. There may not be a road sign here, but turn left and you'll see the "1810 House" on the left, just after the intersection.

In six tenths of a mile, over to your right is a stunning view of the salt marshes with the beach in the distance. You are close to the beach at this point. From here to the beach is downhill now. At the beach there's a large parking lot, dressing rooms, telephone, a little refreshment stand plus one gorgeous beach where you can swim, picnic and/or walk in the dunes.

Come back up the hill, retracing your route. Pass the intersection with Brick Hill Rd. and continue straight on Beach Rd., passing the Raleigh Neck Inn and then, at a "Y" intersection with Main, bear to the right onto Main St. Just before getting to Meeting House Rd. on the right, turn left onto Ministers Rd., which immediately blends into River Rd., and proceed the short distance to Packet Landing, so named from the time, long ago, when packet boots came here from New York and New Jersey on a regular schedule.

Retrace your way back and, at the "Y", bear left, rejoining Main St. where you again turn left. You'll pass the Orleans Arena Theatre and then come to the stop light at the intersection of Main and Tonset. Continue on Main St., crossing Rte. 28 and then 6A. You are passing through the Orleans business district here, with shops of all kinds as you head toward the bay side and Rock Harbor. The road goes gently downhill and in about one and a half miles you arrive at Rock Harbor. This is a tiny, bustling little harbor, chock full of fishing boats—both for professional fishermen and for amateurs who can charter here. A very business-like place with a restaurant and convenient dockside parking lot.

Next, take Rock Harbor Rd. around to the left (a left hand turn, facing inland), and you will soon find yourself paralleling Rte. 6. Just past the Eastham-Orleans town line turn right at the rotary, continuing around it to where a sign says 6A and 28 RIGHT, ORLEANS 1 MILE. Turn right. From here you can see the Inn of the Yankee Fisherman just up ahead and your starting place.

# 15  Eastham - Coast Guard Beach

**Number of miles: 9.7**
**Approximate pedalling time:** 1-½ hours
**Terrain:** Moderately hilly
**Surface:** Good
**Things to see:** Salt Pond Visitors' Center, Eastham Historical Society museum, Eastham Windmill, Great Pond, Nauset Light Beach, Coast Guard Beach, The Outermost House.
**How to get there:** Take Rte. 6 from the north or south into Eastham. Coming from the south, watch for the sign SALT POND VISITORS' CENTER on your right just after the Eastham Town Hall. From the north watch for the sign on your left about one mile after Brackett Rd.

Start the ride in the parking lot of the Salt Pond Visitors' Center where you can leave your "motorized" vehicle, if you have one. There are two of these Visitors' Centers in the National Park Service's Cape Cod National Seashore and both are beautifully designed and integrated architecturally into the landscape. They not only provide you with fascinating information about the human and natural history of the surrounding area through exhibits and illustrated orientation programs, but situated as they are on high ground, they afford marvelous vistas of the seashore.

The Salt Pond Visitors' Center overlooks the quite amazing and beautiful landscape of an enormous salt pond. Plan to spend at least several hours at the Center upon your return. Be sure to explore a bit of the Braille Nature Trail as you leave the parking lot. Cross it near the end of the ride and proceed towards Rte. 6, past the Eastham Historical Society Museum on the right, with its jawbone of a whale gateway. It's open Wednesday and Friday afternoons in July and August.

At Rte. 6, take a left and proceed, using the sidewalk, a short distance to Depot Rd. just across from the Town Hall; turn right. Depot Rd. forms a triangle with, and joins Jemima Pond Rd. Stop and take a look at the Eastham Windmill which is in the triangle. It still works! Proceed down Jemima Pond Rd. past Long Pond on the right to Great Pond Rd.; turn right.

(Continued Page 70)

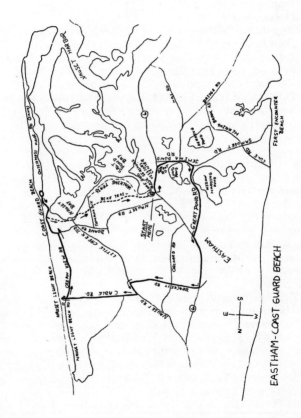

EASTHAM - COAST GUARD BEACH

**Directions for the ride:**

- Start at the Salt Pond Visitors' Center.
- Go west to Rte. 6.
- Turn left on Rte. 6 to Depot Rd.
- Turn right on Depot Rd. to Jemima Pond Rd.
- Turn right on Jemima Pond Rd. to Great Pond Rd.
- Turn right on Great Pond Rd. to Rte. 6.
- Turn left on Rte. 6 to Brackett Rd.
- Turn right on Brackett Rd. to Nauset Rd.
- Turn left on Nauset Rd. to Cable Rd.
- Turn right on Cable Rd. to Nauset Light Beach.
- Return from Nauset Light Beach, west to Ocean View Dr.
- Turn left on Ocean View Dr. to the "T" with Coast Guard Beach Rd.
- Turn left on Coast Guard Beach Rd., up to the beach.
- Take the Bike Path from the right side of the former Coast Guard Station, down to Salt Pond Visitors' Center and your starting place.

If you'd like to take a short side trip to the Cape Cod Bay side, continue straight ahead to First Encounter Beach. Return to Great Pond Rd. and proceed past the Town Landing and public beach on the shore of Great Pond. If you'd like a swim in the warmer waters of a lake, try this one.

Go uphill from Great Pond, continuing on Great Pond Rd. through a residential part of Eastham, back to Rte. 6, about one mile from the turn onto Great Pond from Jemima Pond Rd. When you arrive at Rte. 6, turn left but use the sidewalk on the left because there is a high curb on the opposite side and Rte. 6 is heavily traveled here. In three quarters of a mile, at the stop light at Brackett Rd., there is a large green sign, NAUSET LIGHT BEACH, which is the next destination. Cross Rte. 6 on the light and proceed uphill on Brackett Rd. In about one mile at the "T" intersection with Nauset Rd., turn left, then immediately right onto Cable Rd. to a bluff overlooking the ocean and Nauset Light Beach. The beach is below the bluff and the 114' high steel tower and flashing beacon of the Nauset Beach Light. The light was established in 1838. As you leave Nauset Light Beach parking lot turn left at the first intersection which is Ocean View Dr. When Coast Guard Beach comes into sight, there is a great, sudden downhill, at the bottom of which you must yield, so watch the traffic, then whip up to your left to Coast Guard Beach. Just above the parking lot is the large white building that formerly housed a Coast Guard Station and is now an environmental education center. From the observation area at the side of the house the view is spectacular over the ocean and the tidal wetlands. If you can get back here at sunset, do so; the display of glorious colors is stunning.

At the end of the beach parking lot there's a road going out along the dunes to a tiny two room house called The Outermost House, in which Henry Beston lived and wrote his tender account of a year on the beach, THE OUTERMOST HOUSE, in 1927.

After you have seen and experienced all you have time for, proceed up to the big house and just before the top, you'll see a bike trail that goes down to the right. The trail crosses two spur roads and just before the first one, you'll see the Doane Rock and picnic site. Take this trail and follow it for two delightful miles, mostly downhill, to the Salt Pond Visitors' Center, your starting point.

# 16  South Wellfleet Marconi Station

**Number of miles:** 9.6
**Approximate pedalling time:** 1-½ hours
**Terrain:** Moderately hilly
**Surface:** Very good
**Things to see:** The original Marconi Wireless Station, Marconi Beach, The Audubon Society's Wildlife Sanctuary.
**How to get there:** Proceed out Rte. 6 towards Provincetown, to South Wellfleet. About one and three quarters miles from the Eastham town line, you'll come to the Headquarters of the Cape Cod National Seashore on your right. Turn right and proceed one half mile to the headquarters building parking lot.

Leave your automobile in the parking lot of the Cape Cod National Seashore Headquarters and ride out toward the ocean and the Marconi Station site. This is very flat, almost like a plain. Then the road goes gently uphill to the top of a bluff. Here, on this bluff, Guglielmo Marconi built his wireless station and sent the first wireless telegraph message across the Atlantic to England in 1903, a message from President Teddy Roosevelt to King Edward VII. There is a display that tells the fascinating story. Lock up your bike and take a nature trail to White Cedar Swamp and Forest, crossing the swamp on a boardwalk.

Retrace your road back, past the C.C.N.S. headquarters to the park; turn left and head toward Marconi Beach. This great beach is another of the lovingly preserved, fine white sand beaches of *your* Cape Cod National Seashore, stretching as far as the eye can see. There are bathhouse facilities which are designed low and of weathered grey board to complement, not intrude upon, the landscape. There is a boardwalk with steps leading down to the beach.

When you are ready to continue, return, pass the Headquarters again and proceed to Rte. 6. Turn left onto Rte. 6 and proceed for one and a half miles until you see the white and green sign featuring a herring gull, stating MASS. AUDUBON SOCIETY. Turn right and go straight ahead into the Society's Wellfleet Bay Wildlife Sanctuary. It's open from 8:00 a.m. to 8 p.m. and the fee is one dollar for a bicyclist. When you reach the

(Continued Page 74)

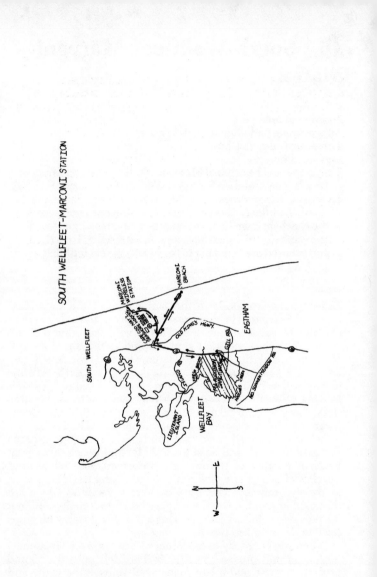

SOUTH WELLFLEET–MARCONI STATION

**Directions for the ride:**

- Start in the parking lot of C.C.N.S. Headquarters.
- Ride east towards the ocean, to the Marconi Station site.
- Return past C.C.N.S. Headquarters to the fork with Marconi Beach Rd.
- Turn left on Marconi Beach Rd. to the Beach.
- Return to the C.C.N.S. road.
- Turn left on the C.C.N.S. road to Rte. 6.
- Turn left on Rte. 6 to the Mass. Audubon Society road.
- Turn right on the Mass. Audubon Society road to the Wildlife Sanctuary.
- Leave the Wildlife Sanctuary on the same road and turn immediately left to Rte. 6.
- Turn left on Rte. 6 to the C.C.N.S. Headquarters road.
- Turn right on the C.C.N.S. road to your starting place.

parking area you'll notice a pipe sticking up out of the ground which has a slot in it—and it is into this pipe that you deposit your fee!

There are picnic tables, rest rooms and a bike road. Try to plan your day so that you have ample time to explore the nature trail on foot. If you go to the office, in the house to your left, you can pick up a map of the Sanctuary. The area that is particularly exciting for nature lovers is Try Island, out in the marsh. Here you can see a landscape that is particularly characteristic of the Cape and of the New England Shore—great tidal wetlands. The island permits you to go out far into the marsh and experience the space, color, smell and rhythm of the wetlands. If you buy guides for the Sanctuary's specific walks, you will be greatly assisted in identifying the rich birdlife and flora of the marsh and woodlands. This is one of the few sites on the Cape which provides access to the wetlands.

When you leave the Sanctuary, turn left at the gate and within a few yards you'll rejoin Rte. 6. Proceed for one mile back to the C.C.N.S. Headquarters. Turn right into the park and in another half-mile you'll reach the parking lot.

# 17 South Wellfleet - Le Count Hollow

Number of miles: 9.7
Approximate pedalling time: 1 hour
Terrain: Definitely hilly
Surface: Good
Things to see: Typical Cape pine forest, Le Count Hollow
   Beach, Ocean View Beach, White Crest Beach, bluffs.
How to get there: Head toward Wellfleet on Rte. 6. Watch for
   the Yum Yum Tree Restaurant on the southeast corner of the
   Rte. 6-Gross Hill Rd. intersection. There is a traffic light and
   a sign saying NEWCOMB HOLLOW-OCEAN BEACH
   Park in the restaurant's parking lot.

Head south down Rte. 6 about one half mile. Just past the
cemetery on your left, turn left on Cahoon Hollow Rd. Go up
hill. It's short but very steep. Take the first right which is Old
King's Hgwy. (This junction lacked a road sign as of this writ-
ing.) You will meander through a semi-residential area of dunes
and a typical Cape pine forest. Old King's Hgwy. is roughly
parallel to Rte. 6. After about a mile and half Bell Rd. comes in
from the right. Continue straight ahead. You will rejoin Rte. 6.
   Turn left on Rte. 6. Go about one quarter of a mile and turn
left on Le Count Hollow Rd. Go straight to the ocean on this
road. Le Count Hollow Beach will be at your feet. This is a
lovely white beach bordered by the Cape's very special green
and blue ocean. You may swim here, or you may prefer to swim
a little further north of here, off Ocean View Ave. where there's
a bit more privacy.
   Head back down Le Count Hollow Rd. for a brief stretch to
Ocean View Ave. Turn right. The crest yields a sensational view
of beach, ocean and the bluffs—dotted with summer cottages
(some for rent; most private). There is a parking lot here. Ride
in, lock your bike and walk down to White Crest Beach. You can
wander on foot all over the bluffs; you'll see numerous trails
heading off through the scrub. Continue going right on Ocean
View Ave. after your swim.
   When Cahoon Hollow Rd. crosses Ocean View you could
detour briefly by taking a right down the steep hill to the Town

(Continued Page 78)

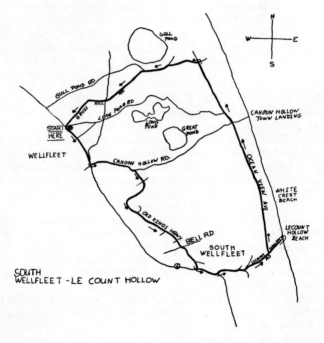

SOUTH
WELLFLEET - LE COUNT HOLLOW

**76**

**Directions for the ride:**

- Park in the Yum Yum Restaurant parking lot on the corner of Rte. 6 and Gross Hill Rd.
- Turn left and south on Rte. 6 to Cahoon Hollow Rd.
- Turn left on Cahoon Hollow Rd. to Old Kings Hgwy.
- Turn right on Old Kings Hgwy. to Rte. 6.
- Turn left on Rte. 6 to Le Count Hollow Rd.
- Turn left on Le Count Hollow Rd. to Le Count Hollow Beach.
- Turn around at the Beach and come back up Le Count Hollow Rd. to Ocean View Ave.
- Turn right on Ocean View Ave. to Gross Hill Rd.
- Turn left on Gross Hill Rd. to Rte. 6 and your starting place.

Landing. If you prefer not to, continue straight for a nice long down downhill giving you stunning views off to your right.

Turn left on Gross Hill Rd. which is very hilly, including a long uphill grade after the fork with Gull Pond Rd. (You continue on Gross Hill Rd.) After about two miles on Gross Hill Rd. you'll return to the intersection and your parking place. Now go inside the Yum-Yum Tree and have a milkshake. (Should their parking lot be too full for parking, you could park at the corner of Rte. 6 and Le Count Hollow Rd. at the shopping Center there, which includes the South Wellfleet Post Office.)

# 18   Wellfleet - Great Island

**Number of miles:** 6.8
**Approximate pedalling time:** 45 minutes
**Terrain:** Hilly
**Surface:** Good
**Things to see:** Wellfleet, Wellfleet Harbor, Mayo Beach,
   Chequesset Neck, Great Island.
**How to get there:** Go toward Wellfleet on Rte. 6. Turn left at
   the traffic light where Rte. 6 crosses a street called Gross Hill
   Rd. going east, and Mill Hill Rd., going west. Follow the sign
   to WELLFLEET CENTER. Park close to the Wellfleet Post
   Office on the corner of West Main St. and Holbrook Ave.


Go east on West Main St., although you might want to visit the
attractive Pisces Gallery and Craftsman's Barn next to the post
office before you start. You'll find Wellfleet an inviting village
to explore on foot as well as by bike.

Take a hairpin turn to the right on East Commercial St. to
head down to Wellfleet Harbor. You will get a fine view of this
large, beautifully protected harbor on your way there. The town
pier at Shirttail Point warrants a stop. Ride out to the end to get
the full effect of the village, the harbor (watched over by a
white, spired church on a hill), and the dunes of Great Island, a
preserve of the Cape Cod National Seashore. At the pier you
may fish or rent a boat.

Upon leaving the pier take Kendrick Ave. west along the
shore. As in every town on the Cape here you'll pass an abundance of guest houses and motels. Bear left at the junction with
Hiller St. which becomes Chequesset Neck Rd. Cross the Herring River. At the top of the hill turn left into the Cape Cod
National Seashore picnic grove and parking area. Here you will
find guides to the hiking trail on Great Island. This trail is an
eight mile round trip which you may want to do provided you
have hiking boots and good health. In any event, walk some
distance onto Great Island just to enjoy the ambience of this
unique natural site. Before returning to town you might want to
go north and downhill on Griffin Island Rd. to the parking area.
Here you can wander along a more remote beach.

To return to town retrace your route along Chequesset Neck
Rd. Bear left staying on Chequesset Neck Rd. at its junction
(Continued Page 82)

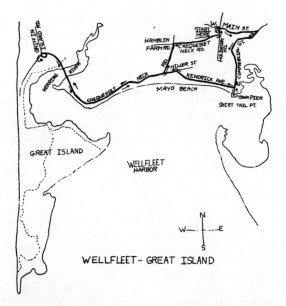

GRIFFIN ISLAND RD.

START HERE

W. MAIN ST.

HAMBLIN FARM RD.

CHEQUESSET NECK RD.

HOLBROOK AVE.

HERRING RIVER

NECK RD.

MILLER ST.

CHEQUESSET NECK

KENDRICK AVE.

COMMERCIAL ST.

MAYO BEACH

TOWN PIER

SHIRT TAIL PT.

GREAT ISLAND

WELLFLEET HARBOR

N
W — E
S

WELLFLEET– GREAT ISLAND

**80**

# 18   Wellfleet - Great Island

**Number of miles: 6.8**
**Approximate pedalling time: 45 minutes**
**Terrain: Hilly**
**Surface: Good**
**Things to see:** Wellfleet, Wellfleet Harbor, Mayo Beach, Chequesset Neck, Great Island.
**How to get there:** Go toward Wellfleet on Rte. 6. Turn left at the traffic light where Rte. 6 crosses a street called Gross Hill Rd. going east, and Mill Hill Rd., going west. Follow the sign to WELLFLEET CENTER. Park close to the Wellfleet Post Office on the corner of West Main St. and Holbrook Ave.

Go east on West Main St., although you might want to visit the attractive Picses Gallery and Craftsman's Barn next to the post office before you start. You'll find Wellfleet an inviting village to explore on foot as well as by bike.

Take a hairpin turn to the right on East Commercial St. to head down to Wellfleet Harbor. You will get a fine view of this large, beautifully protected harbor on your way there. The town pier at Shirttail Point warrants a stop. Ride out to the end to get the full effect of the village, the harbor (watched over by a white, spired church on a hill), and the dunes of Great Island, a preserve of the Cape Cod National Seashore. At the pier you may fish or rent a boat.

Upon leaving the pier take Kendrick Ave. west along the shore. As in every town on the Cape here you'll pass an abundance of guest houses and motels. Bear left at the junction with Hiller St. which becomes Chequesset Neck Rd. Cross the Herring River. At the top of the hill turn left into the Cape Cod National Seashore picnic grove and parking area. Here you will find guides to the hiking trail on Great Island. This trail is an eight mile round trip which you may want to do provided you have hiking boots and good health. In any event, walk some distance onto Great Island just to enjoy the ambience of this unique natural site. Before returning to town you might want to go north and downhill on Griffin Island Rd. to the parking area. Here you can wander along a more remote beach.

To return to town retrace your route along Chequesset Neck Rd. Bear left staying on Chequesset Neck Rd. at its junction

(Continued Page 82)

79

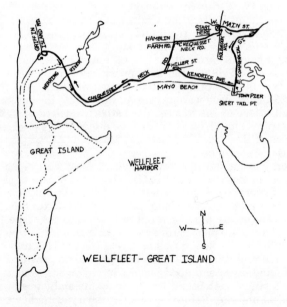

WELLFLEET- GREAT ISLAND

**Directions for the ride:**

- Park close to the Wellfleet Post Office on the corner of West Main St. and Holbrook Ave.
- Go east on W. Main St. to E. Commercial St.
- Turn right on E. Commercial St. to the Town Pier.
- From the Pier turn west on Kendrick Ave. to Hiller St.
- Turn left on Hiller St. to Chequesset Neck Rd.
- Continue straight on Chequesset Neck Rd. to the turnaround at the entrance to Great Island.
- Return on Chequesset Neck Rd. to Holbrook Rd.
- Turn left on Holbrook Rd. to your starting place.

with Hiller St. Chequesset Neck bears sharply right where Hamblin Farm Rd. comes in from your left. Stay on Chequesset Neck Rd. At the "T" intersection with Holbrook Rd. turn left and return to the Wellfleet Post Office on the corner of Holbrook and West Main Sts.

# 19  North Truro - The Highlands

**Number of miles:** 9.8
**Approximate pedalling time:** 1-1/2 hours
**Terrain:** Cape Cod hills
**Surface:** Good
**Things to see:** Head of Meadow Beach; Cape Cod Light, Highland Museum, Jenny Lind Tower, both coasts of the Cape.
**How to get there:** Take Rte. 6 to High Head Rd. which is about five miles from the tip of the Cape at the eastern end of Pilgrim Lake. Turn right going northeast onto High Head Rd. to the small parking lot.

This ride begins at the entrance to the North Truro Bike Trail on High Head Rd. There is a parking lot here tucked away in the dunes at the eastern end of Pilgrim Lake. Leave your car in the parking lot and take off on your bike onto the fine, paved bikes-only trail which wanders through the sand dunes along the edge of Salt Meadow. It runs for a marvelous two miles and comes out at Head of Meadow Beach, onto Head of Meadow Rd. After a visit to the beach, ride down Head of Meadow Rd. When you come to a "Y," continue to the right, towards Rte. 6. When you reach Rte. 6 turn left and then go off Rte. 6 to the right, down a short hill and then left onto Highland Rd. which passes under Rte. 6. You'll see a sign here to HIGHLANDS - 1 MILE.

Highlands means just that, so expect a long incline which levels off in a half mile, then continues up a slight grade to a "T" intersection with a sign saying LIGHTHOUSE and TRURO HISTORICAL MUSEUM. Turn right, go up a short hill, then turn left. You can see the Cape Cod Lighthouse ahead of you. The Highland House Museum is on your left. Run by the Truro Historical Society; it contains every day articles used by the Pilgrims, e.g., fire arms, relics from shipwrecks, etc. It is open from 1:30 p.m. to 4:30 p.m. daily in the summer; a small admission fee is charged. Continue up to the Highland Light (also called the Cape Cod Light). It now flashes a four million candlepower beacon, warning ships, now mostly huge, heavily

(Continued Page 86)

83

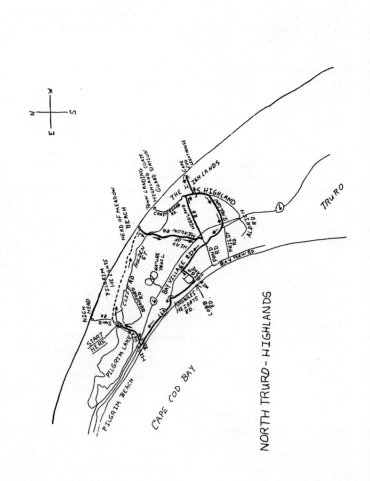

NORTH TRURO – HIGHLANDS

**Directions for the ride:**

- Park in the lot at the entrance to the North Truro Bike Trail.
- Go left onto the Bike Trail to Head of Meadow Rd.
- Go down Head of Meadow Rd. to Rte. 6.
- Turn left onto Rte. 6 to Highland Rd.
- Turn left on Highland Rd. to a "T" intersection.
- Turn right, then left to the Highland Light.
- Return to the intersection with S. Highland Rd.
- Turn left on S. Highland to S. Hollow Rd. to Rte. 6.
- Cross Rte. 6 to 6A.
- Turn right on Rte. 6A to Windigo La.
- Turn left on Windigo La. to Cobb Rd.
- Turn left on Cobb Rd. to Knowles Heights Rd.
- Turn right on Knowles Heights Rd. to Rte. 6A.
- Turn left on 6A to 6.
- Turn left on 6 to High Head Rd.
- Turn right on High Head Rd. to the North Truro Bike Trail parking lot.

laden oil tankers, away from the "Graveyard of Ships." It was originally built in 1797, then destroyed by fire and rebuilt in 1857. From the overlook you can see both sides of the Cape, ocean and bay. As you walk to the overlook you'll see the Jenny Lind Tower—a quirky thing!—and beyond the tower the three radar domes of an Air Force Radar Station. In 1850 Jenny Lind, the "Swedish Nightingale," came to Boston for a concert. More tickets were sold than there were seats. To prevent a riot, Jenny climbed to the top of this tower, so the story goes, and sang to the crowd. In 1927 one Harry Aldrich bought the tower and moved it here.

Retrace your tracks and go down hill to the intersection where you turn left on S. Highland Rd. and run downhill. At the bottom of the grade turn right on S. Hollow Rd. This is a pleasant road, with no houses on either side, which winds its quiet way through stunted pines for a mile, until it comes to Rte. 6. Go across Rte. 6 to the "T" intersection with Rte. 6A, just a few feet from 6, and turn right. This is a pretty stiff uphill for one quarter mile, at which point the road crests and starts to roll up and down.

At approximately one and two tenths miles from your turn onto 6A you'll come to Windigo Lane on the left. Turn left onto it. You are on a bluff; wind around for a short stretch, to Cobb Rd. Turn left onto Cobb and then right where it "Ts" with Knowles Heights Rd. Stay on Knowles Heights Rd. as it wanders for a mile and a half through these dunes, along the Cape Cod Bay shore, until it rejoins 6A at the bottom of the short steep downgrade. Where 6A intersects with Rte. 6, turn left, then right where you see the sign HIGH HEAD. Go up High Head Rd. to the parking lot where you left your car.

# 20  Province Lands

**Number of miles:** 8¾
**Approximate pedalling time:** 1 hour
**Terrain:** Hilly
**Surface:** Excellent
**Things to see:** Herring Cove Beach, spectacular sand dunes, ponds, bogs, Race Point Beach, Province Lands Visitor's Center.
**How to get there:** Take Rte. 6 out to the very end of the Cape. Go around the traffic circle to the Herring Cove Beach parking lot.

This ride is on a specially laid out, asphalt bike path that takes you up and down some spectacular sand dunes and scrub pine forests to the Atlantic Ocean side of the tip of the Cape, then loops back through dramatically contrasting terrain.

When we rode it, in September, after Labor Day, we turned left at the first fork, just past the first underpass under Province Lands Rd., and went clockwise around the circuit. The Cape Cod National Seashore staff recommends a counter-clockwise circuit from this first fork, however. In summer when more bikers are in blossom it is probably wiser to follow their suggestion, although the path is wide enough to pass other bicyclists. There are some great downhills with sharp curves; keep to the right and stay alert.

The area you are passing through was set aside by the "Plimouth Colony" in 1620, a remarkable act on the part of these hardy folk, preoccupied as they must have been with sheer survival.

There are several places to stop and spend some pleasurable time picnicking and/or swimming at either of the two beaches, visiting the Province Lands Visitor's Center, taking the nature walk in the Beach Forest area, or taking a bargain-priced (in 1976) sightseeing flight for $4.00 from the Provincetown Municipal Airport.

The Visitor's Center is up a steep hill from either direction and the panoramic view from its observation deck is breathtaking. There is an outdoor theatre (closed after Labor Day) and inside there are movies about the area and its wildlife every hour on the hour.

(Continued Page 90)

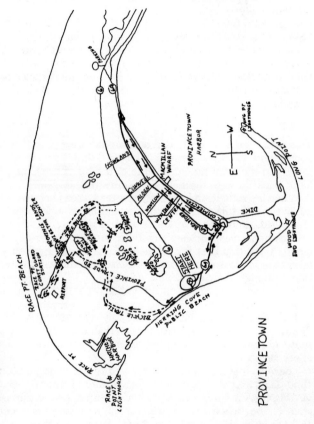

PROVINCELANDS

PROVINCETOWN

RACE PT. BEACH

RACE PT. GUARD
CONSTATION

AIRPORT

PROVINCE LANDS RD.

BICYCLE TRAIL

HERRING COVE
PUBLIC BEACH

RACE PT HARBOR HARBOR

RACE PT

RACE
POINT
LIGHTHOUSE

HOWLANDS

MACMILLAN
WHARF

PROVINCETOWN
HARBOR

COMMERCIAL

ALDEN

BRADFORD

WINSLOW

START
HERE

N
W    E
S

LONG POINT

WOOD
END LIGHTHOUSE

DIKE

LONG PT.
LIGHTHOUSE

88

**Directions for the ride:**

● Park in the Herring Cove Beach parking lot, which is at the left of the building as you face the water. Herring Cove Beach is located at the very tip of Cape Cod at the end of Rte. 6.
● Ride out in front of the building housing the dressing and rest rooms.
● Turn right and ride along the boardwalk to the road that borders the beach here.
● Look for the entrance to the bike path at the very end of the beachside parking, about ½ mile from your start.
● Turn into the bike path and leave the world of automobiles behind.
● Return to the parking lot the same way.

The Beach Forest Trail is a one mile loop that is well worth taking. Be sure you can lock your bike securely before you set out afoot. The walk is beautifully described in detail in SHORT WALKS ON CAPE COD AND THE VINEYARD by Paul and Ruth Sadlier (Pequot Press).

This is one of the nicest rides on the Cape, with short, roller-coaster hills, unique scenery, and *no* automobiles to contend with.

# 21 Provincetown

**Number of miles:** 8.5
**Approximate pedalling time:** 1-1/2 hours
**Terrain:** Slightly hilly
**Surface:** Good
**Things to see:** The myriad wonders of Provincetown! Macmillan
Wharf, Provincetown Aquarium, Playhouse, Pilgrim
Monument and Museum, Seth Nickerson House, Herring
Cove Beach.
**How to get there:** Take Rte. 6 out to the very end of the Cape.
Go around the traffic circle to the Herring Cove Beach
parking lot.

This ride will take you on a tour of fabulous Provincetown with
its old houses, historic landmarks, fishing fleet, and artists and
artisans of all descriptions. After riding from Herring Cove
Beach to the rotary, before you enter the town proper, lock up
your bike and walk out on the dike built to protect Provincetown
Harbor. The dike, which goes over to Long Point, yields a fine
view of the harbor.

The street coming out of Provincetown to this point is one-
way, so you can't use it; instead, continue around the rotary,
retracing your route to the point where 6A heads into town.
Turn right at 6A SOUTH-PROVINCETOWN CENTER-BOS-
TON. This is West Bradford St. There are two principal streets
in Provincetown: Bradford St. which is two-way and Commercial St. which parallels the harbor and is one-way.

As you ride along Bradford, you'll pass numerous little lanes
running between Bradford and Commercial. (You will be returning along the waterfront on Commercial St.) Bradford is
lined with guest houses of all shapes, sizes, and qualities, and
with little restaurants. Pass the David Fairbanks House (1776)
and the Folk Museum. At Winslow St., three miles from the
start of the ride turn left and ride up to the Pilgrim Monument
and Museum.

As you come to the end of Bradford, you'll pass craft shops
such as the Sorcerer's Apprentice and the Artisan's Shop; there
will be dozens more of these on Commercial St. At the junction
with Commercial, make a hairpin turn to the right and head

(Continued Page 94)

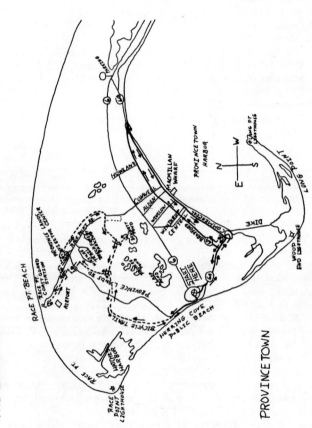

PROVINCELANDS

PROVINCETOWN

**Directions for the ride:**

- Park in the large parking lot at Herring Cove Beach, the one to your left when facing the beach.
- Come out of the lot and bear right.
- Pass Rte. 6 West.
- Continue straight on Rte. 6A towards Provincetown.
- Go straight when 6A goes left, to a rotary at the dike.
- Come back around the rotary to where 6A goes right.
- Turn right on 6A South which is Bradford St., to the junction with Commercial St.
- Turn right onto Commercial and continue to the end of Commercial at the rotary.
- Turn right and go straight to the Herring Cove Beach Parking lot.

back along the waterfront. At this end of town many little cottages are jammed cheek-to-jowl along the road.

About a mile from the Bradford-Commercial intersection, you'll reach the downtown area. There are some older houses sprinkled through the area on the right, as well as such places as the Provincetown Art Association Gallery. Restaurants, galleries and shops are piled on each other. Leatherwork, silverwork, antique jewelry, paintings, prints, portraits done in a single sitting—all are available here. Throngs of pedestrians make riding in this narrow street almost impossible; you'll probably find you'd rather get off your bike and push it along through the center of town—or, lock it up while you stroll here, joining the vacationers in a snack or drink at such places as the Inn at the Mews or the Café Blasé (located next to one of several bike rental stands).

Macmillan Wharf is at the five point mile on the ride. Go out on the wharf to admire the boats. If you can be here at 6:00 a.m. you can watch the commercial fishermen and their catches, and if you have two hours to spare take a cruise on one of the two grand old schooners, HINDU or OLAD. Down past the wharf there are numerous additional crafts people and portrait painters. Soon you'll pass Town Hall Square, the famous Provincetown Playhouse and Union Square with its many shops.

Turn left where Commercial St. goes almost 90° to the left at the six mile point. You'll come to the town landing and Provincetown's oldest house built circa 1746, at #72 Commercial St. The house is open to the public. This end of Commercial St. has a number of quaint, older houses and a generally more conservative atmosphere than elsewhere, since it is a quiet residential area. A lovely inn, the Red Inn, is located here—it's open year round and serves dinner nightly.

You'll come out at the rotary at the dike after six and a half miles. Turn right and continue back toward the car. Contrary to widely held opinion, Cape Cod is not flat, but is generally rolling and includes some very steep hills and bluffs. The ride ends back at Herring Cove Beach at the parking lot.

# 22 Oak Bluffs - Edgartown

Number of miles: 16
Approximate pedalling time: 1 hour 45 minutes
Surface: Fair
Terrain: Flat to moderately hilly
Things to see: Joseph Sylvia State Beach, Bike Trail, Wesleyan
    Grove Campground, State Lobster Hatchery, East Chop,
    Flying Horses, Felix Neck Wildlife Sanctuary, Ocean Park
How to get there: You may start this ride in Edgartown, Oak
    Bluffs or Vineyard Haven. Study the route to find the starting
    point most convenient for you. Coming from Vineyard
    Haven: Take Beach Rd. to Eastville Ave. You may either pick
    up the bike route at this junction, or cross Oak Bluffs at
    Eastville, take Towanicut and Lake Sts. to Bluff Ave. and
    begin the ride at the ferry landing. In Oak Bluffs: Go to end of
    Bluffs Ave. to the ferry landing. From Edgartown: Leave
    town on Main St. (Vineyard Haven Rd.); ride to the
    intersection with Beach Rd. and start the ride at the south
    end of the Bike Trail which parallels Beach Rd.

Begin at the junction of Bluffs Ave. and Seaview Ave., at the
landing for the Woods Hole and Nantucket ferries. Proceed to
the end of Seaview Ave. on N. Bluff. Enjoy the comings and
goings of the sailboats, fishing vessels, and ferries from Hyannis
and Falmouth as they travel in and out of Oak Bluffs Harbor.

Curve around the point on Circuit Ave. Ext. Turn right on
Bluffs Ave. Lock up your bike here and walk uphill on Circuit
Ave. (Bikes are not allowed.) Circuit is Oak Bluff's main street of
shops, galleries and restaurants. Return to Bluffs Ave. At the
intersection is a carousel called with the old term "Flying
Horses," which has been a part of the Oak Bluffs scene since
1884.

Mount up again, head down Bluffs Ave. and turn left o
Central Ave. This little street will take you uphill to Wesleya.
Grove Camp Ground. At the top of the hill bear right on
Montgomery Ave. to come out at Trinity Park Tabernacle
Explore this unique community of narrow streets crowded with
ornate, colorful, tiny cottages. At this site, Baptist and Meth-
odist Camp meetings have been held since 1835. Tenting gave
way to cottages in the middle 1800s. After making the circuit,

(Continued Page 98)

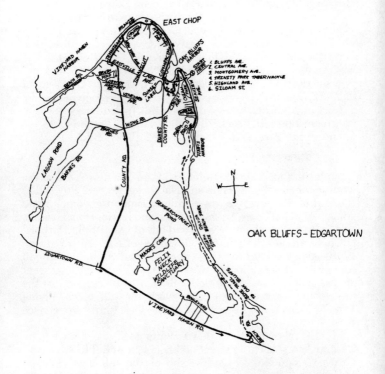

EAST CHOP

VINEYARD HAVEN HARBOR

OAK BLUFFS HARBOR

1. BLUFFS AVE.
2. CENTRAL AVE.
3. MONTGOMERY AVE.
4. TRINITY PARK TABERNACLE
5. HIGHLAND AVE.
6. SILOAM ST.

EASTVILLE AVE.

BEACH RD.

LAGOON POND

BARNES RD.

WING RD.

COUNTY RD.

N
W E
S

SENGEKONTACKET POND

EDGARTOWN RD.

MAJOR'S COVE

FELIX NECK WILDLIFE SANCTUARY

OAK BLUFFS - EDGARTOWN

BOULEVARD

VINEYARD HAVEN RD.

**Directions for the ride:**

- Start from the landing for the Woods Hole and Nantucket ferries in Oak Bluffs.
- Turn right on Seaview Ave. to Circuit Ave. Ext.
- Go around Circuit Ave. Ext. to the left in a loop to Bluffs Ave.
- Turn left on Bluffs Ave. to Central Ave.
- Turn left on Central Ave. to Montgomery Ave.
- Turn right on Montgomery to Highland Ave.
- Turn right on Highland to Siloam Ave.
- Turn right on Siloam to Dukes County Ave.
- Turn right on Dukes County Ave. to Lake Ave.
- Turn left on Lake Ave. to Commercial Ave.
- Turn right on Commercial Ave. which becomes Highland Dr. then Atlantic Ave. to Temahigan Ave.
- Turn right on Temahigan Ave. to Eastville Ave.
- Turn left on Eastville to County Rd.
- Turn right on County Rd. to Edgartown - Vineyard Haven Rd.
- Turn left on Edgartown - Vineyard Haven Rd. to Beach Rd.
- Turn left at the BIKE ROUTE sign just before the Edgartown - Vineyard Haven Rd. and Beach Rd. "Y" intersection and take the Bike Path.
- Follow the Bike Path parallel to Beach Rd. to its end on Seaview Ave.
- Continue on Seaview Ave. to your starting place.

turn right onto Highland Ave. at the foot of Tabernacle Park, and then right again on Siloam Ave. Siloam joins Dukes County Ave. Bear right and proceed to Lake Ave. Sunset Lake is on the left with Lakeside Park on its west side.

Turn left on Lake Ave. and then right on Commercial Ave. Go up onto the bluff and around the point of land called East Chop on Highland Dr. and Atlantic Ave. You'll pass the East Chop Lighthouse and then enjoy a downhill which yields a view of Cape Cod, Vineyard Haven Harbor, West Chop and the West Chop Lighthouse. Your road goes sharply left soon after this and then you turn right on Temahigan Ave.

When Tamahigan "Ts" into Eastville Ave. turn left. The Martha's Vineyard Hospital marks the spot. (Note: This is the junction to Vineyard Haven. If you want to go there, turn right, then left onto Beach St. to cross the causeway. Go over a little drawbridge. Stop at the turnout to take in the activity in Vineyard Haven Harbor on the right and Lagoon Pond on the left.)

Ride east on Eastville Ave. to County Rd. Turn right and head south. In a little less than half a mile you may turn right following the sign to the State Lobster Hatchery. This research facility and hatchery is open to the public.

At the "T" intersection with Edgartown Rd. turn left and head southeast. There are many private roads here which are closed to cars but which bicycles may use if you want to do some exploration.

In about a mile and a half from the turn onto Edgartown Rd., turn left into the Felix Neck Wildlife Sanctuary, a 200 acre tract abutting Segekontacket Pond and comprising marked nature trails.

When you leave Felix Neck, turn left onto Edgartown Rd. In about two miles you'll come to an intersection where Beach Rd. joins Edgartown Rd. from the left. Turn sharply left and north here to start the Bike Trail back to Oak Bluffs. The Trail parallels Beach Rd. for the six mile trip. There is a sign pointing to OAK BLUFFS STATE BEACH. The Bike Trail is paved. Stay on the right! It is not one-way. You'll soon see Sengekontacket Pond on your left and the beach for Edgartown residents on your right. Sylvia (Oak Bluffs) State Beach is a two mile long beach located on this barrier. Stop anywhere for swimming, fishing and picnicking.

Upon leaving the beach, continue north toward Oak Bluffs. About two and a half miles from the State Beach the Bike Trail ends. Continue up the bluffs on Seaview Avenue.

Complete the ride at Ocean Park with its octagonal bandstand and border of gingerbread houses. On summer Sundays a band plays concerts here.

# 23 Chappaquiddick

Number of miles: 7.5
Approximate pedalling time: 1 hour
Surface: Fair
Terrain: Flat to rolling
Things to see: East Beach, Cape Poge Light, Wasque Wildlife
    Preservation Area, Dyke Bridge, ON TIME ferry.
How to get there: Go to the wharf at the end of Main St. in
    Edgartown, turn left on Dock St. and ride to the Town Dock
    which is at the foot of Daggett St.


Get on the tiny ON TIME ferry from Edgartown to Chappaquiddick which plies its brief route continually from 7:30 a.m. until midnight during the season (and until 6:00 p.m. in the off-season). People are charged 25¢ and bikes 30¢ for the trip. It's the greatest transportation bargain around. The passage takes only a *minute*, so savor every *second* of the view of Edgartown, with its elegant Captains' houses and Lighthouse, and of Edgartown Harbor, dotted with boats of all kinds. To your right is Katama Bay. Debark onto Chappaquiddick and proceed straight ahead. There will be many bicycles and they are instructed to KEEP RIGHT. RIDE SINGLE FILE. You'll go by a beach club on the left and Caleb's Inlet on the right. The route goes up an incline. Be sure to pause at the top for the view of Edgartown and its environs. Pass the intersection with School Rd. coming in from the right. Chappaquiddick Rd. becomes Dike Rd. at this point. Now a dirt road, it leads to the famous Dyke Bridge (now a part of American history), East Beach, and Cape Poge. East Beach, about three miles from the ferry landing, is part of the Cape Poge Wildlife Preserve and is a beautiful white sand beach on the Atlantic. A long neck, Cape Poge, extends to the north. Trek out there for privacy, dunes exploration, and to see the Lighthouse and views of Martha's Vineyard. This sand bar protects Cape Poge Bay, as it curves around in an elbow shape. Camping on these beaches is not allowed, but you can spend day after day out here experiencing the sun and the sand (and the mystery of the Chappaquiddick Dyke Bridge). When you leave the beach, retrace your route up the dirt road, past the two houses (which are within a stone's throw of the

(Continued Page 103)

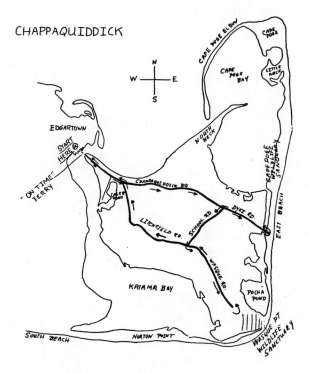

CHAPPAQUIDDICK

START HERE

EDGARTOWN

"ON TIME" FERRY

CALEB POND

CHAPPAQUIDDICK RD

LITCHFIELD RD

SCHOOL RD

DYKE RD

WASQUE RD

NORTH NECK

CAPE POGE ELBOW

CAPE POGE

CAPE POGE BAY

LITTLE NECK

CAPE POGE WILDLIFE SANCTUARY

EAST BEACH

POCHA POND

KATAMA BAY

SOUTH BEACH

NORTON POINT

WASQUE PT WILDLIFE SANCTUARY

101

**Directions for the ride:**

- Take the ON TIME ferry to Chappaquiddick.
- Take Chappaquiddick Rd. to East Beach.
- Turn around and come back to the junction with School Rd.
- Turn left on School Rd.
- Turn left on Wasque Rd.
- Go to Wasque Pt.
- Return and head west on Wasque Rd.
- Continue past the junction with School St. You are now on Litchfield Rd.
- Return to the ferry.

bridge) and the Toms Neck Farm Preserve on the right, which is a commercial shooting range.

Turn left onto School Rd. Turn left onto Wasque Rd. which is a dirt road. Like many roads on Martha's Vineyard, Wasque Rd. has many private roads leading from it. Continue to Wasque Pt. where the one hundred and fifty acre Wasque Reservation is open to the public. Return to the School Rd. junction after exploring Wasque Pt. and continue straight ahead, past School Rd. on what is now Litchfield Rd. (also dirt). Litchfield Rd. rejoins Chappaquiddick Rd. and returns you to the ferry landing.

# 24 Edgartown - Katama (South) Beach

**Number of miles:** 10.5
**Approximate pedalling time:** 1-¼ hours
**Surface:** Fair
**Terrain:** Flat to moderately hilly
**Things to see:** Numerous Captains' houses, Thomas Cooke House Museum, First Federated Church, Edgartown Lighthouse, "ON TIME" ferry, Felix Neck Wildlife Sanctuary, Sheriff's Meadow, Katama (South) Beach.
**How to get there:** Take the Edgartown Rd. from Vineyard Haven or Oak Bluffs or the West Tisbury Rd. from the direction of Gay Head. Take Main St. to the Town Dock.

This ride tours Edgartown and then loops down to Katama Beach and back. It starts at the Town Dock in Edgartown. Go along Dock St. the brief distance between Main and Daggett to the "ON TIME" ferry landing and the Public Wharf. Go up to the observation deck of the wharf for views of Edgartown, the harbor and Chappaquiddick Island, then ride up Daggett St. to North Water St. To your right is the Daggett House Inn built in 1750 and open to the public. Turn right. From here to the end of the street are Martha's Vineyard handsomest Captains' houses. Several were built at an angle to afford views of homebound ships rounding Cape Poge. The chimneys, picket fences, door fans and other well-crafted wood details contributed to the elegance of these houses, built in the early 19th century. The bike route takes you past some but not all of these, so do some additional touring of stately Edgartown if you have time.

At the end of N. Water St., lock up your bike and walk to the Lighthouse, then turn left onto Starbuck Neck Rd. Starbuck Neck Rd. "Ts" into Fuller St. Turn left here and head back toward Main St.

At Morse St. jog right and then immediately left on N. Sumner St. On this street pass the little red brick St. Andrew's Church, the Christine Pease House and the Captain Henry Holt House (1828), now a guest house.

On Main St. turn left, go one block, and then right on S. Water St. Here you'll pass several old, handsome white frame

(Continued Page 107)

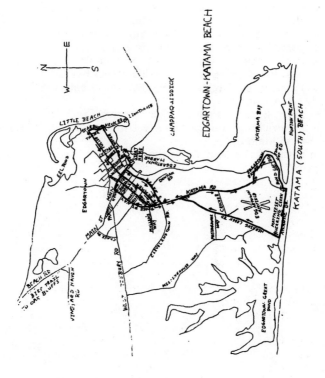

EDGARTOWN-KATAMA BEACH

**Directions for the ride:**

- Start at the Town Dock in Edgartown.
- Go up Daggett St. to N. Water St.
- Turn right on N. Water St. to Starbuck Neck Rd.
- Turn left on Starbuck Neck Rd. to Fuller St.
- Turn left on Fuller St. to Morse St.
- Jog right on Morse, then left on N. Sumner St. to Main St.
- Turn left on Main St. to S. Water St.
- Turn right on S. Water St. to Pease Pt. Way.
- Turn right on Pease Pt. way to School St.
- Turn right on School St. to Main St.
- Turn right on Main St. to S. Sumner St.
- Turn right on S. Sumner St. to Pease Pt. Way.
- Turn left on Pease Pt. Way to Katama Rd.
- Bear left on Katama Rd. to Edgartown Bay Rd.
- Turn left on Edgartown Bay Rd. which becomes Pond Lot Rd. to Atlantic Dr.
- Turn right on Atlantic Dr. to Herring Creek Rd.
- Turn right on Herring Creek Rd. to Katama Rd. to Pease Pt. Way to Main St.
- Turn right on Main St. to the Town Dock, and your starting place.

houses with bright green shutters, all of them of historic interest. These houses form the complex of the Harborside Inn. Proceed on S. Water St. You'll soon see Dunham St. going off to your left; go down Dunham to explore that area if you like; otherwise, proceed to Pease Pt. Way and turn right. Go uphill to School St. and turn right. On the corner of School and Cooke Sts., visit the Thomas Cooke House Museum, then ride back to Main St. (Edgartown's one way streets require lacing back and forth in this manner.)

At Main St. turn right in front of the Courthouse. At S. Sumner St. turn right again. Enjoy the diversity of the shops on Main St. and S. Sumner St. S. Sumner St. has many historically significant buildings, including the First Federated Church (1828) as impressive inside as out, with its box pews, chandeliers, and organ case.

When you return to Pease Pt. Way, turn left and head south to Katama Beach. Your road changes its name to Katama Rd. Bear left at the fork with Edgartown Bay Rd., across from Edgartown air field. At the fork with Town Lot Rd., remain on Edgartown Bay Rd. Circle around the point. The road's name changes to Pond Lot Rd. The barrier beach can be seen from here. Proceed west to rejoin Katama Rd. Turn left heading toward Katama Beach. Your road "Ts" into Atlantic Drive which parallels Mattakesset Herring Creek. Katama Beach is a beautiful three mile long white sand beach. There is surf on the ocean side of the barrier and salt water pond swimming on the Bay side.

When you're ready to leave the area, go west. You'll notice only a few scattered vacation houses and sense a feeling of open space unusual for Martha's Vineyard. Turn right on Herring Creed Rd., ride past the air field and Crocker Rd., and rejoin Katama Rd.

When you cross S. Water St. the road becomes Pease Pt. Way once more. Take it to Main St. At the junction with Main St. you may turn right, going past the Dr. Daniel Fisher House and the Methodist Church, to end your ride at the Town Dock at the foot of Main St.; or, of you would enjoy a side trip to a nature sanctuary, cross Main St. and continue north. Here, Pease Pt. Way is called Planting Field Way, and it will take you directly to Sheriff's Meadow. This eighteen acre wildlife preserve has foot trails through woods and marshlands, including a six mile loop around Eel Pond with Vineyard sound as a backdrop. After your visit retrace your route to Main St. and turn left to reach the Town Dock.

# 25  Vineyard Haven - Lambert's Cove

**Number of Miles:** 15.5
**Approximate pedalling time:** 2 hours
**Surface:** Good
**Terrain:** Hilly
**Things to see:** Vineyard Haven, West Chop, Lambert's Cove
Rd., topsail schooner "Shenandoah," Seamen's Bethel,
Williams Street houses; Cedar Tree Neck
**How to get there:** Take the ferry from Woods Hole to Vineyard
Haven. If you take one of the ferries to Oak Bluffs, follow the
signs to Vineyard Haven.

Start this ride at the ferry landing in Vineyard Haven. If you had
to bring your car, park it in the town parking lot across from the
Steamship Authority lot. Since the island is small and parking
scarce, it would be better to leave your car at Woods Hole and
just bring yourself and your bike.

Facing away from the dock, turn left on Water St. and then
right on Beach St., then go uphill the short distance to Main
where you turn right. Main St. now goes uphill towards West
Chop. As you climb, you can take in all of beautiful Vineyard
Haven Harbor. The hill soon crests and you start a downhill run
of nearly half a mile. At the bottom of the hill Main St. changes
its name to West Chop Ave.

As you go out on the West Chop bluffs the houses get larger.
One mile further on West Chop Ave., which rolls up and down,
you'll notice a BIKE ROUTE sign on the left side of the road. At
the top of West Chop you are overlooking the ocean and your
road goes to the left around the flagpole. The Bike Route, which
you follow, goes around the point in a loop. At the point where
Franklin St. comes in from the right, you continue straight
ahead, following the BIKE ROUTE sign, past the tennis courts
on the left, going uphill beside the playground and tennis
courts. Within a short distance you will have completed the loop
and are back at West Chop Ave. where you turn right.

Come back on West Chop Ave. to Woodlawn Ave., the next
street after the Public Library. You must turn right here because Main is one-way at this point. From Woodlawn turn left

(Continued Page 111)

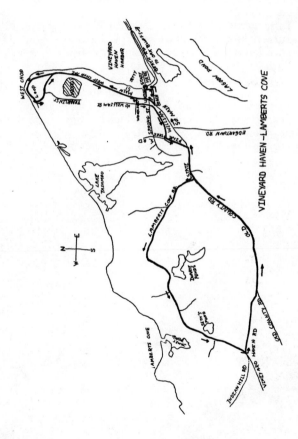

VINEYARD HAVEN—LAMBERTS COVE

**Directions for the ride:**

- Park (or start without a car) on Water St. in front of the Ferry Dock.
- Go left on Water St. to Beach St.
- Turn right on Beach St. to Main St.
- Turn right on Main St. to West Chop Ave. to West Chop itself.
- Loop around West Chop on the Bike Route and return to West Chop Ave.
- Turn right on West Chop Ave. to Woodlawn Ave.
- Turn right on Woodlawn to N. William St.
- Turn left on N. William to Pine Tree Rd.
- Turn left on Pine Tree Rd. to State St.
- Turn right on State St. to Lambert's Cove Rd.
- Turn right on Lambert's Cove Rd. to Vineyard Haven Rd.
- Turn left on Vineyard Haven Rd. to Old County Rd.
- Bear left on Old County Rd. which becomes State St. then S. Main, then Beach, to Water St.
- Turn left on Water St. to your starting place.

onto N. William St. You'll see many beautiful old houses here. Cross Spring St. and follow Williams St. around to the right and uphill, past a handsome yellow and white colonial with black shutters, and several other houses of interest. When you come to the "T" intersection with Pine Tree Rd. turn left. Pine St. then "Ts" into State Rd. at an angle where you turn right heading west, downhill on curving, rolling State Rd.

In six tenths of a mile you come to a turnout on the right with picnic tables and a magnificent view of Lake Tashmoo and the Elizabeth Islands over rolling hills. In less than a half mile you'll see a sign for LAMBERT'S COVE. Turn right at the sign, onto Lambert's Cove Rd. You're now in horse country, with old farms and stone walls and a patch of forest now and again. One mile from the turn onto Lambert's Cove Rd., start a nice downhill run. Just before this hill is the entrance to Cranberry Acres, one of three privately owned campsites open to the public.

In a half mile you pass into West Tisbury and go abruptly uphill, then around a curve and down again. This is a hilly road but very scenic with views of forests and open, flat areas on either side. Pass Duarte Pond on the left and then an old country cemetery on the right. In another four tenths of a mile, start a brief but steep uphill climb to beautiful little Lambert's Cove Methodist Church. Lambert's Cove Rd. curves around to the left, past Seth's Pond and up a four tenths of a mile long grade to the intersection with Vineyard Haven Rd. Take a sharp left turn onto Vineyard Haven Rd. heading back toward Vineyard Haven.

If you are someone who loves to walk along nature trails, you can take a side trip for this intersection by turning right onto Indian Hill Rd. Follow it for three quarters of a mile to the end. Just before the turnaround, a sign on the right directs you to Vineyard Sound. Take this dirt road one mile to the Cedar Tree Neck Wildlife Sanctuary, a three hundred acre sanctuary. No bathing or picnicking is permitted, but, clearly, communing is encouraged.

Continue the ride on Vineyard Haven Rd. Soon Old County Rd. comes in from the right and merges with Vineyard Haven Rd. Bear left and continue on this well paved road which is now taking you through flat countryside. About one and a half miles from this point pass Lambert's Cove Rd. on the left and continue on into Vineyard Haven as Old County Rd. changes to State Rd. and then to S. Main St. as it curves downwards into town. Continue past Main St. to Water St. and turn left to end up where you started from.

# 26  West Tisbury - Menemsha

**Number of miles: 15.5**
**Approximate pedalling time: 2 hours**
**Terrain: Definitely hilly and curving**
**Surface: Fair**
**Things to see:** Menemsha Village Pond and Beach, Village of
West Tisbury, Chilmark Center, seascapes.
**How to get there:** From Vineyard Haven take County Rd. to the
village of West Tisbury, then Music Rd. to Panhandle Rd.
and take Middle Rd. down the center of the island to
Beetlebung Corner.

Start the ride at Beetlebung Corner. ("Beetlebung" is the old
Islander name for the tupelo trees you'll see here.) Go south on
South Rd. The first stretch of the ride is level. It turns sharply
left in a few hundred yards to begin the eastward leg toward
West Tisbury. All along this portion of the ride there will be
views of ponds, hills, the ocean, and the stone walls of old sheep
farms. This is a hilly ride and, combined with the up-island's
typical narrow, curvy roads, it spells caution. In about three
miles a long downhill run offers an expansive view of moors,
dunes and ocean. This will be followed by a gradual uphill grade
before arriving in the village of West Tisbury in about two
miles. A grange Congregational Church, art gallery (with Picas-
soesque sculptures in the garden), and fine old white frame
houses make this an attractive scene. Sir Joshua Slocum who
circumnavigated the globe alone in his sloop, SPRAY, made his
home here for many years before being lost at sea in 1907.

After stopping at the West Tisbury General Store for a candy
bar or an apple continue to the sign VINEYARD HAVEN-7
MILES and turn left, heading north, going past the intersection
with the West Tisbury-Edgartown Rd. Soon there'll be a sharp
left—with a cemetery straight ahead for those who came to
Martha's Vineyard and never left. The terrain is fairly level
along here. Cross Mill Brook enjoying the placid Mill Pond and
its ducks and swans as you pass.

At the fork, bear left up a slight incline on North Rd., following the arrow to MENEMSHA rather than taking the right hand
road to Vineyard Haven. A sign here says BIKE ROUTE. Don't
follow it now, but do follow it later when you take the Martha's

(Continued Page 115)

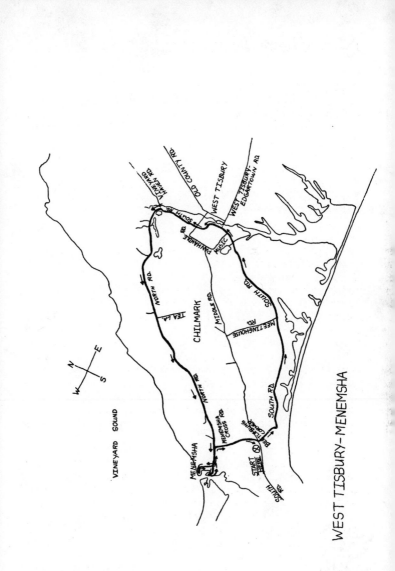

WEST TISBURY-MENEMSHA

**Directions for the ride:**

- Start at Beetlebung Corner.
- Head south on South Rd.
- Go through West Tisbury on South Rd. passing the West Tisbury-Edgartown Rd.
- Bear left onto North Rd., at the fork with Vineyard Haven Rd.
- Pass Tea Lane.
- Enter and tour Menemsha Village.
- Return to North Rd.
- Turn right at Menemsha Cross Rd.
- Return to Beetlebung Corner.

Vineyard State Forest Bike Trail. This lovely curving road goes through wooded areas of trees and thickets but also provides some views of walled pasture land and of Vineyard Sound. In about one and a half miles from the fork, pass Tea Lane, a tree lined narrow dirt road, to your left. It is very beautiful. Explore it if you can. (It goes through to Middle Rd.)

This section of road continues to be quite hilly. About two miles from Tea Lane, the road crests providing a vista of Menemsha Pond. Soon you will go sharply downhill into Menemsha. This is a tiny old fishing hamlet of many docks, fishing shacks clinging to the littoral, small boats, and large fishing vessels. There are boats for charter here and a fine anchorage for visiting pleasure craft. Go on the dirt road along the water front, noticing the Coast Guard station and boat house, then go left to Dutcher's Dock, passing a couple of art galleries, stopping at the tiny Seaboard Snackery for outdoor refreshments, and the village's fish markets where everything from lobster to eels may be purchased fresh daily, on to the public beach which is posted NO DOGS—NO HORSES. From Menemsha Beach you may hike east for a mile to the one hundred and fifty acre Menemsha Hills Reservation for swimming, trail hikes, birding and fishing.

After a swim and stroll, return to North Rd., and go up the steep grade. The intersection with Menemsha Cross Rd. is a half mile from here; turn right onto it and return to Beetlebung Corner passing the handsome Methodist Church, the Fire Station and the Police Station.

# 27 Gay Head

**Number of miles:** 22
**Approximate pedalling time:** 2-3/4 hours
**Surface:** Fair
**Terrain:** Definitely hilly and curving
**Things to see:** Gay Head Cliffs and Lighthouse, Menemsha Pond, Elizabeth Islands.
**How to get there:** From Vineyard Haven and elsewhere on the Island, go west on major roads following signs to Gay Head. Take South Rd. down the center of Gay Head to the Cliffs.

Start your ride at the mile-long Gay Head Cliffs at Martha's Vineyard's westernmost tip. There are public facilities located at the National Historic Landmark, as well as snack bars and souvenir shops. These glacial Cliffs, millions of years old, are made of multi-layered clays of different colors. Paleontologists have uncovered bones of ancient whales, horses, and camels in the area. One couldn't tire of the views afforded from this site: the Cliffs themselves whose clays color the water crashing into them, the western seascape including Cuttyhunk Island and Nomans Land, and the eastern landscape of the lighthouse, the Chillmark hills, and the ponds, dunes and beaches of Martha's Vineyard.

When you leave the Cliffs bear right on the one way loop and then turn right on Moshup Trail. Head downhill toward the water. The Gay Head Town Beach is on the right. Summer houses are perched randomly among the hills and dunes, and the dunes are covered with grasses like bear's fur. Low shrubs, bushes, and stunted trees provide the vegetation at Gay Head. The effect is rather desolate but also unique and therefore arresting.

Oshup Trail parallels the coast. About a mile from the Cliffs Old South Rd. enters from the left. About two miles after this junction a long grade of about seven-tenths of a mile begins. Stop occasionally for resting, and viewing Zachs Cliffs, Long Beach, Squibnocket Pond, and other sights.

At South Rd. turn left. The road soon crests, then continues its up and down formations, continuing to snake as well. At the sign LOBSTERVILLE TOWN BEACH turn right onto Lobsterville Rd. (There used to be a fishing community here of this

(Continued Page 119)

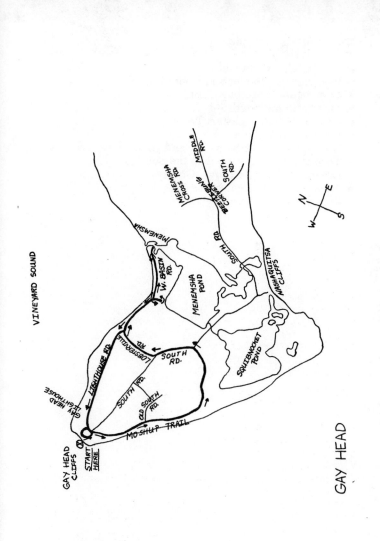

GAY HEAD

**Directions for the ride:**

- Start at Gay Head Cliffs.
- Bear right on the loop in front of the Cliffs.
- Turn right on Moshup Trail.
- Turn left onto South Rd.
- Turn right onto Lobsterville Rd.
- Go past Lighthouse Rd.
- Go right on West Basin Rd. and go to Menemsha Bight.
- Turn around and jog left to the public landing.
- Return to West Basin Rd. Go west.
- Turn right onto Lighthouse Rd.
- Return to the Cliffs.

name.) Enjoy a great downhill ride here as you head toward Vineyard Sound. In a little over a mile, Lighthouse Rd. joins you from the left, but you continue straight ahead and then bear right on West Basin Rd. Follow this road to its end, with Vineyard Sound on your left and Menemsha Pond on your right. An Adriatic-like, pebbly beach is all along this road amid sand dunes. Directly ahead at the end of the road is Menemsha Bight, an inlet of the Sound.

You face the village of Menemsha across the Bight, but—you can't get there from here. (Visit the hamlet on the West Tisbury-Menemsha ride.) Menemsha's harbor is beautifully protected and so is full of fishing and pleasure craft year around.

Turn around and head back up West Basin Rd. Take a brief detour down to the Pond's edge and the public landing where you come upon a road going off to the left. Return to West Basin Rd. and proceed straight ahead to its intersection with Lobsterville and Lighthouse Rd. Head west on Lighthouse Rd. Go uphill. Summer houses also dot the terrain on this side of Gay Head. After about two miles on Lighthouse Rd. you'll arrive at the Gay Head Lighthouse built in 1952. The Lighthouse is automated. The first lighthouse on this site was built in 1799. Continue to the Cliffs and end of your ride there.

# 28  Nantucket Town - Surfside

**Number of miles: 10.2**
**Approximate pedalling time: 2 hours**
**Terrain: Flat to moderately hilly**
**Surface: Good to excellent**
**Things to see:** The marvelous town of Nantucket itself, the
    Folger Museum, The Whaling Museum, Surfside Beach,
    Old Mill, Hawden-Satler House, and the Wharves.
**How to get there:** Take the ferry from Woods Hole or Hyannis.


Start at Steamboat Wharf where the ferry comes in. There are
two bike shops here in case you need supplies or repairs or want
to rent a bike. Go up Broad St. past Easy St. (which is one-way
coming from your left). Ride past Beach St., the Folger
Museum and the Whaling Museum. A visit to both these
museums is definitely in order for a clearer understanding of
Nantucket's past.

Turn left on S. Water St. and then right on Main St. Main is
paved with small, irregular cobblestones dating from the 1830s.
These stones had served as ballast; they were laid to prevent
wagons laden with oil casks from sinking into the sand. They
were a boon in the 1800s but they are a bane to cyclists today.

Go up Main St. to the bank and bear left. Where Gardner
comes in from the right, Main St. goes 45° right, but you bear
left on New Mill St. Pass Vestal on the right. At the fork with
Milk St. bear left on New Mill. The next street is Prospect; turn
left. Watch for street signs. (Since the houses are built close
together, down to the edge of the narrow sidewalks, the street
signs are often hung on the sides of the houses.)

At the fork, bear right onto S. Prospect St. and go about a
quarter of a mile to the intersection of Prospect, Williams,
Sparks and Atlantic Ave. (also called Surfside Rd). The sign says
HOSPITAL and SURFSIDE. Turn almost 90° right onto Atlantic. Within a half mile, you'll see a BIKE PATH sign. Cross over
to it and enjoy a leisurely ride to Surfside Beach. As of the
winter of 1977, the Bike Path did not go all the way to the beach,
but it was expected to be completed by the summer of 1977. It's
a two and a half mile ride to the beach, one of the Island's most
popular, with lifeguard, snack bar and bathhouse.

You can walk for miles in either direction along the South

(Continued Page 123)

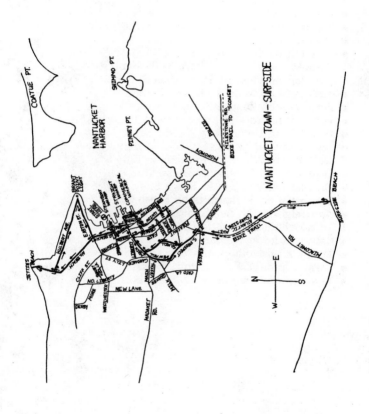

NANTUCKET TOWN-SURFSIDE

**Directions for the ride:**

- Start from Steamboat Wharf in Nantucket Town.
- Go up Broad St. to S. Water St.
- Turn left on S. Water St. to Main St.
- Turn right on Main St. to New Mill St.
- Bear left on New Mill St. to S. Prospect St.
- Turn left on S. Prospect St. to Atlantic (Surfside) Ave.
- Turn right on Atlantic (Surfside) Ave. to the Bike Path.
- Take the Bike Path to Surfside Beach.
- Return from Surfside Beach via the same route to S. Prospect.
- Turn left on S. Prospect to S. Mill St.
- Turn 45° right on S. Mill St. to Pleasant St.
- Turn left on Pleasant St. to Main St.
- Turn right on Main St. to Orange St.
- Turn right on Orange St. to York St.
- Turn left on York St., go one block to Union St.
- Turn left on Union St. to Coffin Dr.
- Turn right on Coffin St. to Washington, to Commercial Wharf to New Whale St. to Main, to Easy St.
- Turn right on Easy St. to Broad St.
- Turn left on Broad to S. Beach St.
- Turn right on S. Beach to N. Beach St.
- Go straight on N. beach St. to Jetties Beach Rd.
- Turn right at the sign to JETTIES BEACH.
- Return as far as Hulbert Ave.
- Turn left on Hulbert Ave. to Easton St.
- Turn right on Easton St. to S. Beach St.
- Turn left on S. Beach St. to Steamboat Wharf.

Shore here. After a surfeit of sun and surf, return along the same route to the Old Mill on the corner of S. Prospect, York and S. Mill Sts.

Turn right around the site of the Old Mill onto S. Mill St. with the Mill on your left. This is the one survivor of the four which originally stood on the hill, grinding corn. Go downhill on S. Mill St. Turn left at the bottom of the hill at the "T" intersection with Pleasant St. Proceed along Pleasant St. to Main where you turn right. On the corner, at 96 Main St., is the Hawden Satler House, the only mansion open to the public. The three Georgian brick mansions across the street are identical. They were built between 1836 and 1838 by William Starbuck, a whaler, for his three sons. The middle house is still inhabited by descendants of the original owner. A Starbuck whaling ship set two records in 1859: It returned with 6,000 barrels of oil after a five year voyage.

At Orange St. turn right. Go as far as York St., just past Dover. More houses of whaling ship captains line Orange St. than any other street in the world. At York St. turn left for a block and then go left on Union St. and head back towards the center of town. At Coffin St. turn right and go to Washington. Turn left, then immediately right heading toward Commercial ("Swain's") Wharf.

Lock your bike to any handy post here and walk around the three public wharves, Commercial, Straight and Old South. Commercial fishing and scalloping boats come and go, as do sail and motor boats of all descriptions.

From here proceed around the parking area on New Whale St., turn up Main, and then go along Easy St. four short blocks to Broad. If you have time for a swim, turn left on Broad and then right onto S. Beach St. Go three blocks to the stop sign at Easton St. Jog across to N. Beach St. Head up a slight hill. Beyond the Bird Sanctuary on the left, bear right where the sign says JETTIES BEACH, the main public beach of the Island. There is a gently sloping beach on one side and a shallow beach for children on the other. The water here is warmer than in most of New England. There is a lifeguard, bathhouse and restaurant.

Leaving Jetties Beach, take the first left, Hulbert Ave. Follow it to Brant Pt. Light. Go right out to the point. Come back and continue straight ahead on Easton to the intersection with N. and S. Beach Sts. Turn left onto S. Beach and proceed back to Steamboat Wharf, your starting place.

# 29 Madaket

**Number of miles: 15.7**
**Approximate pedalling time: 2 hours**
**Terrain: Flat to gently rolling**
**Surface: Very good**
**Things to see:** The western end of Nantucket with its moors, Dionis Beach, Madaket Harbor and Beach, Hither Creek, Eel Point.
**How to get there:** Take the ferry from Woods Hole or Hyannis to Nantucket Town.

Start this ride in front of the Peter Folger Museum on Broad St. and turn right, up the square, past the Pacific National Bank to the Civil War Monument. A sign here points the way to Madaket which is at the western end of the Island. Continue out Main St. which becomes Madaket Rd., a paved road that curves left and right and has a rolling grade. Two miles out from the Civil War Monument, is Eel Point Rd. and a sign reading DIONIS BEACH. Turn right here. Once again you are crossing a tree-less heath.

Within three quarters of a mile you come to a dirt road leading off to the right to DIONIS BEACH. This beach has beautiful sand dunes, a lifeguard, rest rooms and gentle surf (since it is on Nantucket Sound). When you're ready, come back to Madaket Rd. and turn right.

Proceed across the heath (or moor as the Islanders call it). In about two miles cross over an inlet between the two halves of Long Pond, then pass Warren's Landing Rd. on the right. Within a half mile you'll come to Oakland Rd. on the right. Take this down to the water and then turn left. Go as far as you can then turn left again, back up to Madaket Rd. where you turn right. Within three quarters of a mile you come to Madaket Beach which is on the Atlantic side, another splendid beach.

When you come back from the beach turn left and go across the little bridge over the westernmost end of Hither Creek to Smith Point on the left or Jackson Point on the right. Come back to Madaket Rd. and turn left. When you come to a sign saying HITHER CREEK BOATYARD turn left. This is Cambridge St. and it takes you to Little Neck, a Nantucket Conservation

(Continued Page 127)

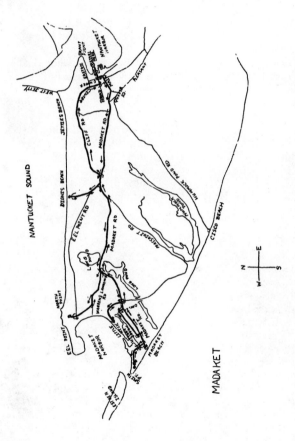

NANTUCKET SOUND

MADAKET

**Directions for the ride:**

- Start on Broad St. and go to S. Water St.
- Turn left on S. Water to Main St.
- Turn right on Main St. to Madaket Rd.
- Bear right on Madaket Rd. to Eel Point Rd.
- Turn right on Eel Point Rd. to Dionis Beach.
- Return from Dionis Beach to Madaket Rd.
- Turn right on Madaket Rd. to Oakland Rd.
- Turn right on Oakland Rd. and then left and left again onto Madaket Rd.
- Turn right back onto Madaket Rd. to Madaket Beach.
- From Madaket Beach come back and turn left, across the little bridge over Hither Creek to Smith Pt.
- Return to Madaket Rd. and turn left to Cambridge St. to Little Neck and then return to Madaket Rd.
- Turn left on Madaket Rd. to Warren's Landing Rd.
- Turn left on Warren's Landing Rd. to Eel Point.
- Return via Warren's Landing Rd. to Madaket Rd.
- Turn left on Madaket Rd. to Cliff Rd.
- Turn left on Cliff Rd. to Center St. to Broad St.
- Turn left on Broad St. to your starting place.

Foundation property open to the public. After exploring this lovely spot, return to Madaket Rd. once more and turn left.

If you have time, you can turn left when you come to Warren's Landing Rd. and take this dirt Rd. out one and a half miles to Eel Point. When you hit the fork with Eel Point Rd. bear right onto Eel Pt. Rd. Eel Point is a 128 acre wildlife reservation where you can bird watch, fish or swim. Coming back to Madaket Rd., turn left once more.

In just under two miles you turn left off of Madaket onto Cliff Rd., just after the road to DIONIS BEACH. Cliff will take you back to Nantucket. Follow it as it curves around to the right and downhill to a fork; bear right, past Lilly St. on the right. This is now Centre St. Take it down to Broad St. Turn left and come back to your starting place.

# 30  Siasconset

Number of miles: 27.2
Approximate pedalling time: 3 hours
Terrain: Flat to moderately hilly
Surface: Good to poor
Things to see: Nantucket Harbor, Wauwinet, Sankaty Head
Light, Sconset and Sconset Beach.
How to get there: Take the ferry to Nantucket from Woods Hole
or Hyannis.


Start this ride at the foot of Main St. in front of the Pacific Club.
In 1859, a group of former whaling ship captains who had sailed
the Pacific formed the Club for "yarning" together.

Walk up the square (because of the cobblestones); just before
reaching the Pacific National Bank turn left onto Orange St.

One mile from the start you come to the Milestone rotary. Go
around to the left, onto Milestone Rd. Almost immediately you
will see a sign to MONOMOY ROAD LEFT - SIASCONSET
STRAIGHT AHEAD. Turn left onto the Monomoy Rd. At the
"T" turn left and follow Boston Ave. This is a dead end road;
retrace your path back to the fork. Bear right on Monomoy Rd.
back to Milestone Rd. Turn left. Very quickly you come to a "Y".
Turn left onto Polpis Rd. at the sign to POLPIS - WAUWINET.

You are now getting your first look at Nantucket's open heath
or moors with their great variety of wildflowers, bayberry,
scrub oak, pine groves and purple scotch heather. The first
settlers found a tree-less island. The Coffin brothers imported
30,000 pine trees in 1851 and planted them in these outlying
areas. Soon you come to the Life Saving Museum on the left,
and then Altar Rock Rd. on the right, with Quaise Rd. on the
left. Both are dirt roads. Take a side trip out to Quaise or Altar
Rock. (Each is a one mile round trip.) Quaise is the area the
original owner of Nantucket, Thomas Mayhew, kept when he
sold the rest in 1659. Altar Rock is the highest point on the
Island.

About five miles out you come to a dirt road on the left which
runs a quarter of a mile out to Polpis Harbor, another tiny
settlement. Keep a sharp eye out for this road; it's easy to miss.
Immediately after it is the paved road to Wauwinet. Turn left
onto the road. After two gently rolling miles, you will see the

(Continued Page 131)

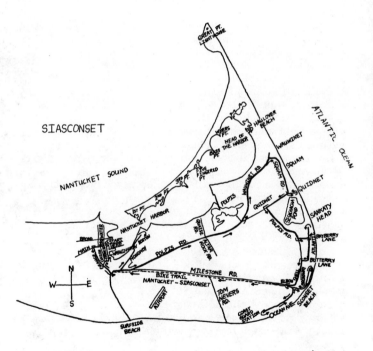

SIASCONSET

ATLANTIC OCEAN

NANTUCKET SOUND

NANTUCKET HARBOR

GREAT PT. LIGHTHOUSE

HALLOWER BEACH

WAUWINET

SQUAM

QUIDNET

SANKATY HEAD

SURFSIDE BEACH

MILESTONE RD.

BIKE TRAIL
NANTUCKET - SIASCONSET

TOM NEVERS RD.

AIRPORT

COAST GUARD STATION

OCEAN AVE.

SCONSET BEACH

BUTTERFLY LANE

BAYBERRY LANE

POLPIS RD.

N
W — E
S

129

**Directions for the ride:**

- Start at the foot of Main St. in Nantucket in front of the Pacific Club and go up Main St. to Orange St.
- Turn left on Orange to Milestone Rd.
- Bear left on Milestone Rd. to Monomoy Rd.
- Turn left on Monomoy Rd. to Boston Rd.
- Turn left on Boston to the end; turn around and come back to Monomoy Rd. and to Milestone Rd.
- Turn left on Milestone Rd. to Polpis Rd.
- Turn left on Polpis Rd. to Wauwinet Rd.
- Turn left on Wauwinet Rd. to the end.
- Return on Wauwinet to Squam Rd.
- Turn left on Squam Rd. to Quidnet Rd.
- Turn right on Quidnet Rd. to Polpis Rd.
- Turn left on Polpis Rd. to Bayberry Lane.
- Turn left on Bayberry Lane to Atlantic Ave.
- Turn left on Atlantic and go to the end, then return on Atlantic to Butterfly Lane.
- Turn right on Butterfly Lane to Polpis Rd.
- Turn left on Polpis to Shell.
- Bear right on Shell to Elbow Lane.
- Turn right on Elbow Lane to the rotary.
- Go around the flagpole and around to the right, uphill to Ocean Ave.
- Bear right on Ocean Ave. (also called Beach Rd.) to the Coast Guard Loran Station.
- Turn around and go back to just before the rotary, turn $100°$ right and down under the footbridge to 'Sconset Beach.
- Return uphill to the rotary to Milestone Rd.
- Go on Milestone Rd. to the Bike Path.
- Take the Bike Path alongside Milestone Rd. all the way to Milestone Rotary then go to Orange St.
- Take Orange St. to Union St.
- Turn right on Union to Francis St.
- Turn right on Francis and then left onto Washington St.
- Take Washington back to your starting place.

Squam Rd. on the right; continue straight a short distance until you arrive at the Refuge Reception Station. Check in at the Reception Station and ride or walk the short distance to the beach. To the left is the section at the head of the harbor, called the Haulover, named for the custom of the early fisherman hauling their dories over the sand from the harbor to the ocean.

Come back to Squam Rd. and turn left; ride one and a half miles on this narrow dirt road, with the ocean on the left and Squam Swamp on the right, to the point where Quidnet Rd. (paved) comes in from the right. Continue straight ahead and then left to Quidnet, another tiny summer cottage settlement. Come back to Quidnet Rd. and turn left onto it. Ride for a mile and then come back to Polpis Rd. Turn left. You will come out on the shore of Sesachacha Pond. Soon you can see the Sankaty Head Lighthouse. About eight tenths of a mile from Hicks Hollow Rd. you'll come to Bayberry Lane. Turn left and go to Atlantic Ave. Turn left, out to the lighthouse, then come back and continue on Atlantic down to Butterfly Lane where you turn right, then left on Polpis Rd.

Immediately you will come to the sign that says SIASCON-SET. Bear left. You are now in the village of 'Sconset with its doll sized cottages. These originally were fishing shacks which were then enlarged to their present size when the women of the fishermen decided to join them here.

At the "Y", of Broadway and Shell Sts., bear right on Shell. Turn right on Elbow Lane to the rotary (with the flagpole made from a ship's spar). Go around to the left and then right, uphill on Ocean Ave., also called Beach Rd., which goes along a bluff. After a short ride, turn around at the Coast Guard Loran Station and go back. Just before the rotary take a hairpin turn downhill and around to the right, under the footbridge to 'Sconset Beach.

The road down here makes a loop so you have to go back up the way you came. Go under the footbridge to the rotary. Turn left onto Milestone Rd. Look for the sign for the Bike Path, which starts a half mile from the rotary. Take the bike path straight back to Nantucket Town. The bike path ends just before the Milestone Rotary; turn right on Orange St. When you get to Union St., turn right and follow it around to Francis St. on the right. Turn right and then left onto Washington which skirts South Beach.

At the point where Washington bears left at the fork with Candle St. (which is one way the wrong way), you may bear left and return to Main St., *or* turn right onto Commercial (or "Swain's") Wharf to tour the wharf area before ending your ride.

# Notes